THE
NATURE
— OF —
FLORIDA

AN INTRODUCTION TO FAMILIAR PLANTS, ANIMALS & OUTSTANDING NATURAL ATTRACTIONS

WATERFORD PRESS

THE
NATURE
—— OF ——
FLORIDA

AN INTRODUCTION TO FAMILIAR PLANTS, ANIMALS & OUTSTANDING NATURAL ATTRACTIONS

By James Kavanagh

Illustrations by Raymond Leung
Introduction by James C. Rettie

WATERFORD PRESS

Publisher's Cataloging in Publication Data
Kavanagh, James Daniel, 1960 -
The Nature of Florida. An Introduction to Familiar Plants, Animals & Outstanding Natural Attractions (2nd ed). Includes bibliographical references and index.
1. Natural History – Florida. 2. Animals – Identification – Florida.
3. Plants – Identification – Florida. 4. Tourism – Florida.

Library of Congress Catalog Card Number: 2005936119
ISBN 10: 1-58355-302-9
ISBN 13: 978-1-58355-302-2

The introductory essay, "BUT A WATCH IN THE NIGHT" by JAMES C. RETTIE is from FOREVER THE LAND by RUSSELL AND KATE LORD. Copyright © 1950 by Harper & Brothers, copyright renewed © 1978 by Russell and Kate Lord. Reprinted with permission of HarperCollins Publishers.

The author would like to acknowledge the following institutions and individuals who contributed to the research and development of this guide:
>   The Florida Department of Tourism
>   The Florida Game & Fresh Water Commission
>   The United States Geological Survey
>   The U.S. Fish & Wildlife Service
>   The U.S. Forest Service
>   National Parks Service
>   Tim Jacox   Diane Dufresne
>   Joe Thomas   Tina Oma
>   David Nickerson

The maps in this guide are adapted from maps copyright © by the United States Geological Survey and are reproduced with permission.

Waterford Press' toll-free order/information line is (800) 434-2555.
Download product information from our website: **www.waterfordpress.com**

While every attempt has been made to ensure the accuracy of the information in this guide, it is important to note that experts often disagree with one another regarding the common name, size, appearance, habitat, distribution and taxonomy of species. For permissions, or to share comments, e-mail editor@waterfordpress.com.

CONTENTS

To my sisters,

Sandy, Carol, Dolly & Jo

The Nature of Florida is intended to provide novice naturalists with a pocket reference to the state's familiar and distinctive species of plants and animals and the outstanding natural attractions found in Florida.

The guide's primary purpose is to introduce the reader to common plants and animals and to highlight the diversity of species found in Florida. Its secondary purpose is to show how all species in each ecosystem found here – from the tundra to alpine forests – depend on each other, directly and indirectly, for survival.

Environmental education begins when individuals learn to appreciate the plants and animals in their immediate environment. When they start to care about local species – which often begins by learning their names – they take the first step toward understanding their place (as an animal) within an ecosystem.

The guide opens with a brief introduction to evolution. This is not intended in any way to dispute creationism, but is merely intended to illustrate the similarities and differences between major groups of plants and animals and show when each appeared in geologic time. To study the fossil record is fascinating in and of itself, but one of the most stunning things it reveals is a number of transitional species that are intermediary between different classes of organisms.

The brilliant introductory essay by James C. Rettie provides a simplified view of the evolution of life on earth, and the role that man – the animal – has played to date.

J.D.K.

BUT A WATCH IN THE NIGHT

BY JAMES C. RETTIE

James C. Rettie wrote the following essay while working for the National Forest Service in 1948. In a flash of brilliance, he converted the statistics from an existing government pamphlet on soil erosion into an analogy for the ages.

OUT BEYOND OUR SOLAR SYSTEM there is a planet called Copernicus. It came into existence some four or five billion years before the birth of our earth. In due course of time it became inhabited by a race of intelligent men.

About 750 million years ago the Copernicans had developed the motion picture machine to a point well in advance of the stage that we have reached. Most of the cameras that we now use in motion picture work are geared to take twenty-four pictures per second on a continuous strip of film. When such film is run through a projector, it throws a series of images on the screen and these change with a rapidity that gives the visual impression of normal movement. If a motion is too swift for the human eye to see it in detail, it can be captured and artificially slowed down by means of the slow-motion camera. This one is geared to take many more shots per second – ninety-six or even more than that. When the slow motion film is projected at the normal speed of twenty-four pictures per second, we can see just how the jumping horse goes over a hurdle.

What about motion that is too slow to be seen by the human eye? That problem has been solved by the use of the time-lapse camera. In this one, the shutter is geared to take only one shot per second, or one per minute, or even one per hour – depending upon the kind of movement that is being photographed. When the time-lapse film is projected at the normal speed of twenty-four pictures per second, it is possible to see a bean sprout growing up out of the ground. Time-lapse films are useful in the study of many types of motion too slow to be observed by the unaided, human eye.

The Copernicans, it seems, had time-lapse cameras some 757 million years ago and they also had superpowered telescopes that gave them a clear view of what was happening upon this earth. They decided to make a film record of the life history of earth and to make it on the scale of one picture per year. The photography has been in progress during the last 757 million years.

In the near future, a Copernican interstellar expedition will arrive upon our earth and bring with it a copy of the time-lapse film. Arrangements will be made for showing the entire film in one continuous run. This will begin at midnight of New Year's eve and continue day and night without a single stop until midnight on December 31. The rate of projection will be 24 pictures per second. Time on the screen will thus seem to move at the rate of twenty-four years per second; 1440 years per minute; 86,400 years per hour; approximately two million years per day and sixty-two million years per month. The normal lifespan of individual man will occupy about three seconds. The full period of earth history that will be unfolded on the screen (some 757 million years) will extend from what the geologists call the Pre-Cambrian times up to the present. This will, by no means, cover the full time-span of the earth's geological history but it will embrace the period since the advent of living organisms.

During the months of January, February, and March the picture will be desolate and dreary. The shape of the land masses and the oceans will bear little or no resemblance to those that we know. The violence of geological erosion will be much in evidence. Rains will pour down on the land and promptly go booming down to the seas. There will be no clear streams anywhere except where the rains fall upon hard rock. Everywhere on the steeper ground the stream channels will be filled with boulders hurled down by rushing waters. Raging torrents and dry stream beds will keep alternating in quick succession. High mountains will seem to melt like so much butter in the sun. The shifting of land into the seas, later to be thrust up as new mountains, will be going on at a grand scale.

Early in April there will be some indication of the presence of single-celled living organisms in some of the warmer and sheltered coastal waters. By the end of the month it will be noticed that some of these organisms have become multicellular. A few of them, including the Trilobites, will be encased in hard shells.

Toward the end of May, the first vertebrates will appear, but they will still be aquatic creatures. In June about 60 percent of the land area that we know as North America will be under water. One broad channel will occupy the space where the Rocky Mountains now stand. Great deposits of limestone will be forming under some of the shallower seas. Oil and gas deposits will be in process of formation – also under shallow seas. On land there will be no sign of vegetation. Erosion will be rampant, tearing loose particles and chunks of rock and grinding them into sand and silt to be spewed out by the streams into bays and estuaries.

About the middle of July the first land plants will appear and take up the tremendous job of soil building. Slowly, very slowly, the mat of vegetation will spread, always battling for its life against the power of erosion. Almost foot by foot, the plant life will advance, lacing down with its root structures whatever pulverized rock material it can find. Leaves and stems will be giving added protection against the loss of the soil foothold. The increasing vegetation will pave the way for the land animals that will live upon it.

Early in August the seas will be teeming with fish. This will be what geologists call the Devonian period. Some of the races of these fish will be breathing by means of lung tissue instead of through gill tissues. Before the month is over, some of the lung fish will go ashore and take on a crude lizard-like appearance. Here are the first amphibians.

In early September the insects will put in their appearance. Some will look like huge dragonflies and will have a wing span of 24 inches. Large portions of the land masses will now be covered with heavy vegetation that will include the primitive spore-propagating trees. Layer upon layer of this plant growth will build up, later to appear as coal deposits. About the middle of this month, there will be evidence of the first seed-bearing plants and the first reptiles. Heretofore, the land animals will have been amphibians that could reproduce their kind only by depositing a soft egg mass in quiet waters. The reptiles will be shown to be freed from the aquatic bond because they can reproduce by means of a shelled egg in which the embryo and its nurturing liquids are sealed and thus protected from destructive evaporation. Before September is over, the first dinosaurs will be seen – creatures destined to dominate the animal realm for about 140 million years and then to disappear.

In October there will be series of mountain uplifts along what is now the eastern coast of the United States. A creature with feathered limbs – half bird and half reptile in appearance – will take itself into the air. Some small and rather unpretentious animals will be seen to bring forth their young in a form that is a miniature replica of the parents and to feed these young on milk secreted by mammary glands in the female parent. The emergence of this mammalian form of animal life will be recognized as one of the great events in geologic time. October will also witness the high-water mark of the dinosaurs – creatures ranging in size from that of the modern goat to monsters like Brontosaurus that weighed some 40 tons. Most of them will be placid vegetarians, but a few will be hideous-looking carnivores, like Allosaurus and Tyrannosaurus. Some of the herbivorous dinosaurs will be clad in bony armor for protection against their flesh-eating comrades.

November will bring pictures of a sea extending from the Gulf of Mexico to the Arctic in space now occupied by the Rocky Mountains. A few of the reptiles will take to the air on bat-like wings. One of these, called Pteranodon, will have a wingspread of 15 feet. There will be a rapid development of the modern flowering plants, modern trees, and modern insects. The dinosaurs will disappear. Toward the end of the month there will be a tremendous land disturbance in which the Rocky Mountains will rise out of the sea to assume a dominating place in the North American landscape.

As the picture runs on into December it will show the mammals in command of the animal life. Seed-bearing trees and grasses will have covered most of the land with a heavy mantle of vegetation. Only the areas newly thrust up from the sea will be barren. Most of the streams will be crystal clear. The turmoil of geological erosion will be confined to localized areas. About December 25 will begin the cutting of the Grand Canyon of the Colorado River. Grinding down through layer after layer of sedimentary strata, this stream will finally expose deposits laid down in Pre-Cambrian times. Thus in the walls of that canyon will appear geological formations dating from recent times to the period when the earth had no living organisms upon it.

The picture will run on through the latter days of December and even up to its final day with still no sign of mankind. The spectators will become alarmed in the fear that man has somehow been left out. But not so; sometime about noon on December 31 (one million years ago) will appear a stooped, massive creature of man-like proportions. This will be Pithecanthropus, the Java ape man. For tools and weapons he will have nothing but crude stone and wooden clubs. His children will live a precarious existence threatened on the one side by hostile animals and on the other by tremendous climatic changes. Ice sheets – in places 4,000 feet deep – will form in the northern parts of North America and Eurasia. Four times this glacial ice will push southward to cover half the continents. With each advance the plant and animal life will be swept under or pushed southward. With each recession of the ice, life will struggle to re-establish itself in the wake of the retreating glaciers. The woolly mammoth, the musk ox, and the caribou all will fight to maintain themselves near the ice line. Sometimes they will be caught and put into cold storage – skin, flesh, blood, bones, and all.

The picture will run on through supper time with still very little evidence of man's presence on earth. It will be about 11 o'clock when Neanderthal man appears. Another half hour will go by before the appearance of Cro-Magnon man living in caves and painting crude animal pictures on the walls of his dwelling. Fifteen minutes more will bring Neolithic man, knowing how to chip stone and thus produce sharp cutting edges for spears and tools. In a few minutes more it will appear that man has domesticated the dog, the sheep and, possibly, other animals. He will then begin the use of milk. He will also learn the arts of basket weaving and the making of pottery and dugout canoes.

The dawn of civilization will not come until about five or six minutes before the end of the picture. The story of the Egyptians, the Babylonians, the Greeks, and the Romans will unroll during the fourth, the third, and the second minute before the end. At 58 minutes and 43 seconds past 11:00 P.M. (just 1 minute and 17 seconds before the end) will come the beginning of the Christian era. Columbus will discover the new world 20 seconds before the end.

The Declaration of Independence will be signed just 7 seconds before the final curtain comes down.

In those few moments of geologic time will be the story of all that has happened since we became a nation. And what a story it will be! A human swarm will sweep across the face of the continent and take it away from the [Native Americans]. They will change it far more radically than it has ever been changed before in a comparable time. The great virgin forests will be seen going down before ax and fire. The soil, covered for eons by its protective mantle of trees and grasses, will be laid bare to the ravages of water and wind erosion. Streams that had been flowing clear will, once again, take up a load of silt and push it toward the seas. Humus and mineral salts, both vital elements of productive soil, will be seen to vanish at a terrifying rate.

The railroads and highways and cities that will spring up may divert attention, but they cannot cover up the blight of man's recent activities. In great sections of Asia, it will be seen that man must utilize cow dung and every scrap of available straw or grass for fuel to cook his food. The forests that once provided wood for this purpose will be gone without a trace. The use of these agricultural wastes for fuel, in place of returning them to the land, will be leading to increasing soil impoverishment. Here and there will be seen a dust storm darkening the landscape over an area a thousand miles across. Man-creatures will be shown counting their wealth in terms of bits of printed paper representing other bits of a scarce but comparatively useless yellow metal that is kept buried in strong vaults. Meanwhile, the soil, the only real wealth that can keep mankind alive on the face of this earth is savagely being cut loose from its ancient moorings and washed into the seven seas.

We have just arrived upon this earth. How long will we stay?

Because this guide has been written for the novice, every attempt has been made to simplify presentation of the material. Illustrations are accompanied by brief descriptions of key features, and technical terms have been held to a minimum. Plants and animals are arranged more-or-less in their taxonomic groupings. Exceptions have been made when nontraditional groupings facilitate field identification for the novice (e.g., wildflowers are grouped by color).

SPECIES DESCRIPTION

The species descriptions have been fragmented to simplify presentation of information:

① **ROSEATE SPOONBILL**
② *Ajaia ajaja*
③ **Size:** To 32 in. (80 cm)
④ **Description:** White-pinkish wading bird has unique bill with a flattened, spoon-shaped tip.
⑤ **Habitat:** Mangrove keys, estuaries, mudflats, lagoons.
⑥ **Comments:** It swings its bill from side to side in shallow water while feeding on small fish, crustaceans and insects. They fly with their legs and necks outstretched.

① **COMMON NAME**
The name in bold type indicates the common name of the species. It is important to note that a single species may have many common names.

② *Scientific Name*
The italicized latin words refer to an organism's scientific name, a universally accepted two-part term that precisely defines its relationship to other organisms. The first capitalized word, the genus, refers to groups of closely related organisms. The second term, the species name, refers to organisms that look similar and interbreed freely. If the second word in the term is 'spp.', this indicates there are several species in the genus that look similar to the one illustrated. If a third word appears in the term, it identifies a subspecies, a group of individuals that are even more closely related.

③ **Size**
Generally indicates the maximum length of animals (nose to tail tip) and the maximum height of plants. Exceptions are noted in the text.

④ **Description**
Refers to key markings and/or characteristics that help to distinguish a species.

⑤ **Habitat**
Where a species lives/can be found.

⑥ **Comments**
General information regarding distinctive behaviors, diet, vocalizations, related species, etc.

ILLUSTRATIONS

The majority of animal illustrations show the adult male in its breeding coloration. Plant illustrations are designed to highlight the characteristics that are most conspicuous in the field. It is important to note that illustrations are merely meant as guidelines; coloration, size and shape will vary depending on age, sex or season.

SPECIES CHECKLISTS

The species checklists at the back of this book are provided to allow you to keep track of the plants and animals you identify.

TIPS ON FIELD IDENTIFICATION

Identifying a species in the field can be as simple as one, two, three:

1. Note key markings, characteristics and/or behaviors;
2. Find an illustration that matches; and
3. Read the text to confirm your sighting.

Identifying mammals or birds in the field is not fundamentally different than identifying trees, flowers or other forms of life. It is simply a matter of knowing what to look for. Reading the introductory text to each section will make you aware of key characteristics of each group and allow you to use the guide more effectively in the field.

N.B. – *We refer primarily to familiar species in this guide and do not list all species within any group. References listed in the bibliography at the back of this guide provide more detailed information about specific areas of study.*

EVOLUTION OF ANIMALS

WHAT IS AN ANIMAL?

Animals are living organisms which can generally be distinguished from plants in four ways:

1. They feed on plants and other animals;
2. They have a nervous system;
3. They can move freely and are not rooted; and
4. Their cells do not have rigid walls or contain chlorophyll.

All animals are members of the animal kingdom, a group consisting of more than a million species. Species are classified within the animal kingdom according to their evolutionary relationships to one another.

Most of the animals discussed in this guide are members of the group called vertebrates. They all possess backbones and most have complex brains and highly developed senses.

The earliest vertebrates appeared in the oceans about 500 million years ago. Today, surviving species are divided into five main groups:

1. Fishes
2. Amphibians
3. Reptiles
4. Birds
5. Mammals

Following is a simplified description of the evolution of the vertebrates and the differences between groups.

FISHES

The oldest form of vertebrate life, fishes evolved from invertebrate sea creatures 400-500 million years ago. All are cold-blooded (ectothermic) and their activity levels are largely influenced by the surrounding environment.

The first species were armored and jawless and fed by filtering tiny organisms from water and mud. Surviving members of this group include lampreys and hagfishes. Jawless fishes were succeeded by jawed fishes that quickly came to dominate the seas, and still do today. The major surviving groups include:

1. **Sharks and rays** – more primitive species that possess soft skeletons made of cartilage; and
2. **Bony fishes** – a more advanced group of fishes that have bony skeletons, it includes most of the fishes currently existing.

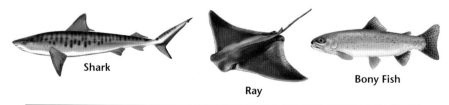

Shark

Ray

Bony Fish

Physiological Characteristics of Fishes

- **Heart and gills**
A two-chambered heart circulates the blood through a simple system of arteries and veins. Gills act like lungs and allow fishes to absorb dissolved oxygen from the water into their bloodstream.

- **Nervous system**
Small anterior brain is connected to a spinal cord which runs the length of the body.

- **Digestive system**
Digestive system is complete. A number of specialized organs produce enzymes which help to break down food in the stomach and intestines. Kidneys extract urine from the blood and waste is eliminated through the anus.

- **Reproduction**
In most fishes, the female lays numerous eggs in water and the male fertilizes them externally. Young usually hatch as larvae, and the larval period ranges from a few hours to several years. Survival rate of young is low.

- **Senses**
Most have the senses of taste, touch, smell, hearing and sight, although their vision is generally poor. Fishes hear and feel by sensing vibrations and temperature and pressure changes in the surrounding water.

AMPHIBIANS

The first limbed land-dwellers, amphibians evolved from fishes 300-400 million years ago and became the dominant land vertebrates for more than 100 million years. Like fishes, amphibians are cold-blooded and their activity levels are largely influenced by the environment.

The first fish-like amphibian ancestors to escape the water were those that had the ability to breathe air and possessed strong, paired fins that allowed them to wriggle onto mud-flats and sandbars. (Living relics of this group include five species of lungfish and the rare coelacanth.) Although amphibians were able to exploit rich new habitats on land, they remained largely dependent on aquatic environments for survival and reproduction.

The major surviving groups are:

1. **Salamanders** – slender-bodied, short-legged, long-tailed creatures that live secretive lives in dark, damp areas; and
2. **Frogs and toads** – squat-bodied animals with long hind legs, large heads and large eyes. Frogs are smooth skinned, toads have warty skin.

Salamander

Frog

Toad

Advances Made Over Fishes

- **Lungs and legs**
  By developing lungs and legs, amphibians freed themselves from the competition for food in aquatic environments and were able to flourish on land.

- **Improved circulatory system**
  Amphibians evolved a heart with three chambers that enhanced gas exchange in the lungs and provided body tissues with highly oxygenated blood.

- **Ears**
  Frogs and toads developed external ears that enhanced their hearing ability, an essential adaptation for surviving on land.

- **Reproduction**
  Most amphibians reproduced like fish. Salamanders differ in that most fertilize eggs internally rather than externally. In many, the male produced a sperm packet which the female collected and used to fertilize eggs as they were laid.

REPTILES

Reptiles appeared 300-350 million years ago. They soon came to dominate the earth, and continued to rule the land, sea and air for more than 130 million years. Cold-blooded like amphibians, reptiles evolved a host of characteristics that made them better suited for life on land.

About 65 million years ago, the dominant reptiles mysteriously underwent a mass extinction. A popular theory suggests this was caused by a giant meteor hitting the earth which sent up a huge dust cloud that blotted out the sun. The lack of sun and subsequently low temperatures caused many plants and animals to perish.

The major surviving reptilian groups are:

1. **Turtles** – hard-shelled reptiles with short legs;
2. **Lizards** – scaly-skinned reptiles with long legs and tails;
3. **Snakes** – long, legless reptiles with scaly skin; and
4. **Crocodilians** – very large reptiles with elongate snouts, toothy jaws and long tails.

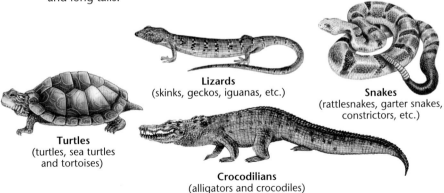

Lizards
(skinks, geckos, iguanas, etc.)

Snakes
(rattlesnakes, garter snakes, constrictors, etc.)

Turtles
(turtles, sea turtles and tortoises)

Crocodilians
(alligators and crocodiles)

Advances Made Over Amphibians

- **Dry, scaly skin**
  Their dry skin prevents water loss and also protects them from predators.

- **Posture**
  Many reptiles evolved an upright posture and strong legs which enhanced their mobility on land.

- **Improved heart and lungs**
  Their heart and lungs were more efficient which heightened their activity levels. The heart had four chambers – although the division between ventricles was usually incomplete – making it less likely that oxygenated and deoxygenated blood would mix.

- **Defense**
  They were agile and better able to defend themselves, having sharp claws and teeth or beaks capable of inflicting wounds.

BIRDS

Birds evolved from reptiles 100-200 million years ago. Unlike species before them, birds were warm-blooded (endothermic) and able to regulate their body temperature internally.* This meant that they could maintain high activity levels despite fluctuations in environmental temperature. They are believed to have evolved from a group of gliding reptiles, with their scaly legs considered proof of their reptilian heritage.

Birds come in a vast array of groups. All have feathered bodies, beaks, lack teeth and have forelimbs modified into wings. Most can fly.

Advances Made Over Reptiles

- **Ability to fly**
  By evolving flight, birds were able to exploit environments that were inaccessible to their competitors and predators. The characteristics they evolved that allowed them to fly included wings, feathers, hollow bones and an enhanced breathing capacity.

- **Warm-blooded**
  An insulating layer of feathers enhanced their capacity to retain heat. They also had true four-chambered hearts that enhanced their ability to maintain high activity levels in varying environments.

- **Keen senses**
  Birds evolved very keen senses of vision and hearing and developed complex behavioral and communicative patterns.

- **Reproduction**
  Fertilization was internal and the eggs had hard, rather than leathery, shells. Unlike most reptiles, birds incubated their eggs themselves and protected and nurtured their young for a period of time following birth.

* There is still a debate over whether or not some dinosaurs were warm-blooded.

MAMMALS

Mammals evolved from reptiles 100-200 million years ago. Though warm-blooded like birds, they are believed to have different reptilian ancestors. In addition to being warm-blooded, mammals also evolved physiological adaptations which allowed them to hunt prey and avoid predation better than their competitors.

Mammals quickly exploited the habitats left vacant by the dinosaurs and have been the dominant land vertebrates for the past 65 million years. Man is a relatively new addition to the group, having a lineage of less than 3 million years.

Mammals have evolved into three distinct groups, all of which have living representatives:

1. **Monotremes** – egg-laying mammals;
2. **Marsupials** – pouched mammals which bear living, embryonic young; and
3. **Placentals** – mammals which bear fully-developed young.

Monotremes
(platypus and echidna)

Marsupials
(opossums, kangaroos etc.)

Placentals
(squirrels, humans, dogs, rats etc.)

Advances Made Over Birds

- **Reproduction**
  Fertilization was internal, but in most, the young developed in the female's uterus instead of an egg. After birth, the young were fed and nurtured by adults for an extensive period, during which they learned behavioral lessons from their elders and siblings. This emphasis on learned responses at an early age is believed to have contributed to the superior intelligence and reproductive success of the group.

- **Hearing**
  Most had three bones in the middle ear to enhance hearing. (Birds and reptiles have one.)

- **Teeth**
  Many developed specialized teeth that allowed them to rely on a variety of food sources. Incisors were for cutting, canines for tearing and molars for chewing or shearing.

- **Breathing**
  Mammals evolved a diaphragm which increased breathing efficiency.

- **Posture**
  Many evolved long, strong legs and were very agile on land.

EVOLUTION OF PLANTS

WHAT IS A PLANT?

Plants are living organisms which can generally be distinguished from animals in four ways:

1. They synthesize their own food needed for maintenance and growth from carbon dioxide, water and sunlight;
2. They do not have a nervous system;
3. Most are rooted and cannot move around easily; and
4. Their cells have rigid walls and contain chlorophyll, a pigment needed for photosynthesis.

All plants are members of the plant kingdom. According to the fossil record, plants evolved from algae that originated nearly 3 billion years ago. Since then, plants have evolved into millions of species in a mind-boggling assortment of groups.

Most North American plants are classified into two main groups:

1. **Gymnosperms** – plants with naked seeds; and
2. **Angiosperms** – flowering plants with enclosed seeds.

Gymnosperms   Angiosperms

GYMNOSPERMS – THE NAKED SEED PLANTS

This group of mostly evergreen trees and shrubs includes some of the largest and oldest known plants. They began to appear around 300-400 million years ago, and were the dominant plant species on earth for nearly 200 million years. The most successful surviving group of gymnosperms are the conifers, which include such species as pines, spruces, firs, larches and junipers.

Most conifers are evergreen and have small needle-like or scale-like leaves which are adapted to withstand extreme temperature changes. Some species are deciduous, but most retain their leaves for two or more years before shedding them.

Reproduction

Most conifers produce cones – wood-like fruits that contain the male and female gametes. The male cones produce pollen that is carried by the wind to settle between the scales of female cones on other trees. The pollen stimulates ovules to change into seeds, and the scales of the female cone close up to protect the seeds. When the seeds are ripe, up to two years later, environmental conditions stimulate the cone to open its scales and the naked seeds to fall to the ground.

ANGIOSPERMS – THE FLOWERING PLANTS

Angiosperms first appeared in the fossil record around 130 million years ago. They quickly adapted to a wide variety of environments and succeeded gymnosperms as the dominant land plants. Their reproductive success was largely due to two key adaptations:

Advances Made Over Gymnosperms

1. They produced flowers which attracted pollinating agents such as insects and birds; and
2. They produced seeds encased in fruits to aid in seed dispersal.

Angiosperms are classified in two main groups:

1. **Monocots** – plants with one embryonic leaf at germination, parallel-veined leaves, stems with scattered vascular bundles with little or no cambium (group includes grasses, cattails, orchids and corn); and
2. **Dicots** – plants with two embryonic leaves at germination, net-veined leaves, stems with cylindrical vascular bundles in a regular pattern that contain cambium (group includes more than 200,000 species ranging from tiny herbs to huge trees).

Angiosperms make up a diverse and widespread group of plants ranging from trees and shrubs such as oaks, cherries, maples, hazelnuts and apples, to typical flowers like lilies, orchids, roses, daisies, and violets. The trees and shrubs within this group are commonly referred to as deciduous and most shed their leaves annually.

Reproduction

A typical flower has colorful petals that encircle the male and female reproductive structures (see illustration p. 127). The male stamens are composed of thin filaments supporting anthers containing pollen. The female pistil contains unfertilized seeds in the swollen basal part called the ovary. Pollination occurs when pollen, carried by the wind or animals, reaches the pistil.

Once fertilization has occurred, the ovules develop into seeds and the ovary into a fruit. The fruit and seeds mature together, with the fruit ripening to the point where the seeds are capable of germinating. At maturity, each seed contains an embryo and a food supply to nourish it upon germination. Upon ripening, the fruit may fall to the ground with the seeds still inside, as in peaches, cherries and squash, or it may burst open and scatter its seeds in the wind, like poplar trees, willows and dandelions.

Fruit comes in many forms, from grapes, tomatoes, apples and pears, to pea and bean pods, nuts, burrs and capsules. Regardless of its shape, fruit enhances the reproductive success of angiosperms in two important ways. First, it helps to protect the seeds from the elements until they have fully matured, enabling them to survive unfavorable conditions. Secondly, fruit aids in seed dispersal. Some fruits are eaten by animals that eventually release the seeds in their feces, an ideal growing medium. Others may be spiny or burred so they catch on the coats of animals, or may have special features which enable them to be carried away from their parent plant by the wind or water.

GEOLOGICAL TIMESCALE

ERA	PERIOD	MYA*	EVENTS
CENOZOIC	HOLOCENE	.01	Dominance of man.
	QUATERNARY	2.5	First human civilizations.
	TERTIARY	65	Mammals, birds, insects and angiosperms dominate the land.
MESOZOIC	CRETACEOUS	135	Dinosaurs extinct. Mammals, insects and angiosperms undergo great expansion. Gymnosperms decline.
	JURASSIC	190	Age of Reptiles; dinosaurs dominant. First birds appear.
	TRIASSIC	225	First dinosaurs and mammals appear. Gymnosperms are dominant plants.
PALEOZOIC	PERMIAN	280	Great expansion of reptiles causes amphibians to decline. Many marine invertebrates become extinct.
	CARBONIFEROUS	340	Age of Amphibians; amphibians dominant. First reptiles appear. Fish undergo a great expansion.
	DEVONIAN	400	Age of Fishes; fishes dominant. First amphibians, insects and gymnosperms appear.
	SILURIAN	430	First jawed fishes appear. Plants move onto land.
	ORDOVICIAN	500	First vertebrates appear.
	CAMBRIAN	600	Marine invertebrates and algae abundant.

*Millions of years ago

Prominent Lakes and Rivers

GEOGRAPHY

Area: 58,560 sq. mi. (94,240 sq. km)
Peak Elevation: 345 ft. (105 m) in Walton County
Tidal Coastline: 8,462 mi. (13,617 km)

Florida is a relatively flat, lowland plain that arose from the ocean a mere 25 million years ago. It is surrounded on three sides by water, and all places in the state are within 70 miles (110 km) of salt water.

Outstanding Features

Beaches

Florida has more coastline than any other state except Alaska and more than 800 miles (1,287 km) of beaches. The beaches and nearshore areas are inhabited by hundreds of species of mollusks and crustaceans, and shell collecting is a popular activity throughout the state. The state's pristine white beaches are composed of quartz sand that is constantly scrubbed by wave action.

Lakes & Rivers

Florida has more than 7,800 lakes and 1,700 rivers and streams. The 730 sq. mi. (1,126 sq. km) Lake Okeechobee is the fourth largest lake in the U.S. Major waterways include the St. Johns, Apalachicola, Kissimmee, and Suwannee rivers.

Aquifers & Springs

Florida is underlain by a thick sedimentary crust composed primarily of sand and limestone. Over the years, this porous rock was broken down by rains that eroded huge underground cavities (aquifers) and channels (springs). Today, the aquifers act like huge rain barrels that store much of the state's fresh water. The water is discharged to the surface via springs. There are numerous spring-fed sinkhole lakes in Florida, many of which periodically disappear when subsurface water levels fluctuate.

Islands

Thousands of islands are found off Florida's meandering coastline, and more than 4,500 are 10 acres (4 ha) or larger in size. The most notable groups of islands are the Florida Keys that extend from Biscayne Bay near Miami 135 miles (217 km) into the Gulf of Mexico.

Coral Reefs

The coral reefs in southern Florida harbor the greatest diversity of marine life found anywhere in the U.S. The John Pennekamp Coral Reef State Park off the Florida Keys protects a portion of the only living coral reef in the continental U.S.

Dominant Vegetation Types

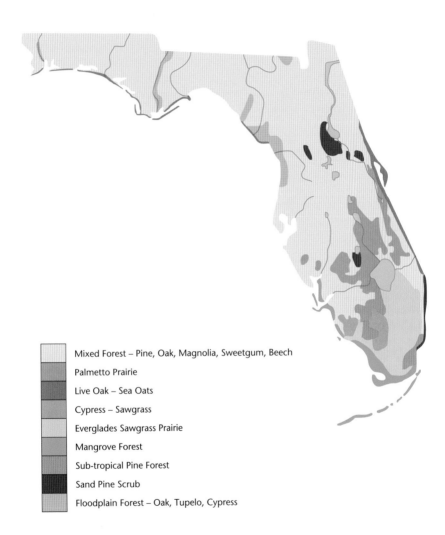

Mixed Forest – Pine, Oak, Magnolia, Sweetgum, Beech
Palmetto Prairie
Live Oak – Sea Oats
Cypress – Sawgrass
Everglades Sawgrass Prairie
Mangrove Forest
Sub-tropical Pine Forest
Sand Pine Scrub
Floodplain Forest – Oak, Tupelo, Cypress

NATURAL VEGETATION

Florida's variable soils and habitats support a huge diversity of plants, many of which are found only in Florida (endemic species). About 2,500 of the 6,000 plants that grow in Florida are native to the state.

The state has more than 300 species of trees – nearly half of all the species found in the U.S. Some of the most familiar species include pines, oaks, palms, palmettos, sweetgums, beeches, mangroves, maples and magnolias. The map at the left illustrates the dominant vegetation types in different areas of the state.

The most common terrestrial habitat in Florida is **pine flatwoods** – open flat areas supporting pine forests with an understory of palmettos, shrubs and grasses. Flatwoods located on different kinds of soil support different species of pines, with the most familiar species being longleaf, slash, loblolly and sand pine.

Wildflowers are ubiquitous and bloom throughout the year. Species range from run-of-the-mill weeds to carnivorous pitcher plants and bladderworts, floating plants like lilies and hyacinths, and air plants (bromeliads) like wild pine that live on trees and derive their nourishment from air and rainwater.

Florida has many low-lying areas that are saturated with water and are designated as **wetlands**. The state's two major wetland areas are the Everglades region, which encompasses the southern tip of peninsular Florida, and the Okefenokee Swamp which stretches from the Osceola National Forest into Georgia.

The wet prairie of the Everglades is dotted with 'tree islands' that grow on elevated areas where soil has been able to accumulate. Called **hammocks** by locals, they support unique populations of trees, shrubs and grasses and serve as dry refuges for Everglades wildlife.

Florida also has **dry prairies**, vast treeless areas found between woodlands, waterways and wet areas. These unique, dry habitats are home to many endangered and threatened species including the burrowing owl, whooping and sandhill cranes and the crested caracara. The most famous dry prairie in the state is Payne's Prairie near Gainesville, home to 800 species of plants and 350 species of animals.

The sandy forests of the '**Big Scrub**' in the north-central part of the state are another uniquely Floridian habitat. Here are the only places where forests of endemic sand pine grow. It is called a scrub area, since many of the trees and the understory plants including palmetto, oaks and shrubs grow stunted in the poor soil.

WHAT ARE MAMMALS?

Most mammals are warm-blooded, furred creatures that have 4 limbs and a tail, 5 digits on each foot, and several different kinds of teeth. All North American species give birth to live young which feed on milk from their mother's mammary glands.

HOW TO IDENTIFY MAMMALS

Mammals are generally secretive in their habits and therefore difficult to spot in the field. The best time to look for mammals is at dusk, dawn and at night, since many retreat to burrows during the day to escape the heat. Some of the best places to look for them are in undisturbed areas affording some source of cover such as wood edges and scrub thickets.

When you spot a mammal, consider its size, shape and color. Check for distinguishing field marks and note the surrounding habitat.

COMMON TRACKS

Studying tracks is an easy way to discover the kinds of mammals found in your area. For more information on animal tracks, see the references under mammals in the back of the guide.

Mouse Opossum Squirrel Raccoon

Skunk Eastern Cottontail Bobcat Armadillo

Gray Fox Wild Boar White-tailed Deer Black Bear

N.B. – *Tracks are not to scale*

MARSUPIALS

Related to kangaroos and koala bears, the opossum is the only marsupial found in North America. Young are born prematurely and move to a fur-lined pouch (marsupium) where they complete their development attached to a teat.

VIRGINIA OPOSSUM
Didelphis virginiana
Size: To 40 in. (1 m)
Description: Distinguished by its long, grayish fur, white face, black-tipped ears and naked, rat-like tail.
Habitat: Woodlands, farming areas, forest edges.
Comments: Most active in the evening and at night, it is the only mammal in the U.S. that has a grasping (prehensile) tail. It has the peculiar habit of pretending to be dead (playing possum) when frightened.

ARMADILLOS

The armadillo belongs to a group of mammals that includes sloths and anteaters.

NINE-BANDED ARMADILLO
Dasypus novemcinctus
Size: To 32 in. (80 cm)
Description: Cat-sized mammal is covered with an armored coat consisting of bony plates covered with thin scales.
Habitat: Woodlands, scrubby areas, along streams.
Comments: Like the opossum, it often forages near roadways at night and many are killed by automobiles. During the day it rests in underground burrows. When threatened, armadillos may roll into a ball or burrow rapidly. Also called pocket dinosaurs, Hoover hogs and Texas turkeys.

INSECTIVORES

Insectivores are animals that eat insects. They are generally small, with long snouts, short legs and sharp teeth.

EASTERN MOLE
Scalopus aquaticus
Size: To 9 in. (23 cm)
Description: Brownish mammal with a pointed snout and a short naked tail. Front feet have out-turned palms and long claws.
Habitat: Loose soils in a variety of rural and urban habitats.
Comments: Presence can be detected by the mounds of dirt it pushes up when tunneling underground. An expert digger, it can disappear underground in a matter of seconds.

LEAST SHREW
Cryptotis parva
Size: To 4 in. (10 cm)
Description: Mouse-like creature with a long, pointed nose, a short tail and gray to brown fur.
Habitat: Woodlands, farming areas, forest edges.
Comments: Most active in the evening and at night. One of 3 shrews found in Florida.

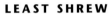

BATS

The only true flying mammals, bats have large ears, small eyes and broad wings. Primarily nocturnal, they have developed a sophisticated sonar system – echolocation – to help them hunt insects at night. During daylight, they seek refuge in caves, trees and attics. Rarely harmful, bats are valuable in helping check insect populations. 16 species are found in Florida.

SOUTHEASTERN BAT
Myotis austroriparius
Size: To 4 in. (10 cm)
Description: Dark brown bat with woolly fur. Underparts are buff-colored.
Habitat: Roosts primarily in caves where water is abundant.
Comments: Colonies of up to 90,000 individuals gather together in caves during spring breeding season.

BRAZILIAN FREE-TAILED BAT

Tadarida brasiliensis
Size: To 5 in. (13 cm)
Description: Brown bat is distinguished by its tail which sticks out beyond the tail membrane.
Habitat: Roosts primarily in caves.
Comments: Likely the most common bat in Florida, it nests in huge colonies. 'Clouds' of bats can be seen emerging from roosting sites to feed on insects at dusk.

RABBITS & ALLIES

Members of this distinctive group of mammals have long ears, large eyes and long hind legs. Primarily nocturnal, they commonly rest in protected areas such as thickets during the day. When threatened, they thump their hind feet on the ground as an alarm signal.

EASTERN COTTONTAIL

Sylvilagus floridanus
Size: To 18 in. (45 cm)
Description: Gray-brown bunny with a white, cottony tail. Nape of neck is rust-colored.
Habitat: Thick brushy areas, fields.
Comments: Feeds primarily on grass. Most active at dawn and dusk, it rests in thickets during the day. Females have up to 7 litters a year of 1-9 young.

MARSH RABBIT

Sylvilagus palustris
Size: To 18 in. (45 cm)
Description: Darker than the cottontail, it has short ears, small, reddish feet and an inconspicuous, dark tail.
Habitat: Swamps, borders of lakes and waterways.
Comments: May take to water when panicked and swim with only its nose and eyes exposed. Has the unusual habit of occasionally walking on two legs.

SQUIRRELS

This diverse family of hairy-tailed, large-eyed rodents includes chipmunks, tree squirrels, ground squirrels and marmots. All but the tree squirrels live in burrows on or under the ground throughout the year. Most are active during the day and are easily observed in the field. Size includes tail length.

EASTERN GRAY SQUIRREL
Sciurus carolinensis
Size: To 20 in. (50 cm)
Description: Gray squirrel with buff-colored highlights on its face, back and sides. White and beige phases are also found in Florida.
Habitat: Wooded areas throughout Florida.
Comments: Florida's most common mammal, it nests in trees and feeds on a wide variety of nuts, seeds, berries and acorns. Most active in morning and evening.

FOX SQUIRREL
Sciurus niger
Size: To 28 in. (70 cm)
Description: Large squirrel has a long bushy tail with yellow-tipped hairs. Coloration is highly variable, ranging from gray-and-black to brown-and-black.
Habitat: Mixed and coniferous forests, swamps.
Comments: Eats mostly nuts, seeds and acorns. Once abundant, its population has declined drastically in recent years due to habitat loss.

SOUTHERN FLYING SQUIRREL
Glaucomys volans
Size: To 10 in. (25 cm)
Description: Large-eyed squirrel is gray above and light below. Note loose skin fold along its sides.
Habitat: Forested areas.
Comments: Capable of gliding distances of over 200 ft. (61 m) by spreading its limbs and stretching its flight skin taut. A nocturnal species, it can be heard thumping about in the dark while foraging.

POCKET GOPHERS

These mole-like mammals are well known for the mounds of dirt they push up when excavating their burrows. They are named for their fur-lined, external cheek pouches that they stuff with food or nesting material.

SOUTHEASTERN POCKET GOPHER
Geomys pinetis
Size: To 13 in. (33 cm)
Description: Distinguished by its brownish coat, huge front feet and long, crescent-shaped claws. Unlike the eastern mole, it has visible eyes.
Habitat: Sandy soils in northern Florida.
Comments: Feeds on tubers, roots and other vegetation. Also known as salamanders and sandy-mounders.

MICE & ALLIES

The members of this huge group of rodents differ greatly in form and habits, though most have large ears, long tails and breed throughout the year. Dedicated omnivores, they have adapted to practically every North American habitat.

COTTON MOUSE
Peromyscus gossypinus
Size: To 8 in. (20 cm)
Description: Coat is tawny-brown above and white below. Slightly haired tail is about half of its body length.
Habitat: Wooded areas, swamps, beaches.
Comments: One of Florida's most abundant mammals, it is a strong swimmer and a skillful climber.

HOUSE MOUSE
Mus musculus
Size: To 8 in. (20 cm)
Description: Gray to brown mouse with large eyes and ears and a long, naked tail.
Habitat: Buildings, human dwellings, cultivated fields.
Comments: An introduced species common throughout Florida. Females have up to 14 litters of 3-16 young annually.

FLORIDA WOODRAT
Neotoma floridana
Size: To 16 in. (40 cm)
Description: Coat is gray-brown above and white below. Long tail is bicolored.
Habitat: Marshes, low woodlands with a dense understory.
Comments: Builds elaborate 'houses' made of sticks – 2-5 ft. (60-150 cm) high – that are often built around a rock or fallen log. In the fall it collects seeds and nuts and stores them in its home. Also called packrats, woodrats have a penchant for shiny objects discarded by people.

Black Rat

BLACK RAT
Rattus rattus
Size: To 18 in. (45 cm)
Description: Black or brownish rodent with a long scaly tail.
Habitat: Seaports, buildings.
Comments: Like the house mouse, this species was inadvertently introduced from Europe and is now widespread in North America. Often nests in palm trees. Its brownish cousin, the Norway rat (*R. norvegicus*) is also found in Florida.

Norway Rat

FLORIDA WATER RAT
Neofiber alleni
Size: To 15 in. (38 cm)
Description: Glossy brown aquatic rodent with a long, rounded tail.
Habitat: Swamps, marshes, lakes, streams.
Comments: Also called a round-tailed muskrat, it builds feeding platforms in shallow water where it dines on swamp vegetation. Nests in small dome-shaped houses constructed from grasses.

HISPID COTTON RAT
Sigmodon hispidus
Size: To 14 in. (35 cm)
Description: Brown to black rat with coarse, grizzled fur. Tail is less than half the total body length.
Habitat: Meadows, farmlands, ditches.
Comments: Extremely prolific, it begins breeding at six weeks old. One of the most common mammals in Florida and the most common rodent in the southeastern U.S., it is a major crop pest.

NUTRIA

Introduced from South America for fur-farming, Nutrias are now widespread and outcompete many native species for food and habitats. They also cause considerable crop damage in Florida.

NUTRIA
Myocastor coypus
Size: To 4 ft. (1.2 m)
Description: Large brown aquatic rodent with a long round tail.
Habitat: Marshes, streams, ponds.
Comments: It often feeds on land and, once disturbed, enters the water with a loud splash.

RACCOONS & ALLIES

The raccoon belongs to a family of mammals which includes the coati of Central and South America and the lesser panda of Asia.

COMMON RACCOON
Procyon lotor
Size: To 3 ft. (90 cm)
Description: Easily distinguished by its black mask and ringed tail.
Habitat: Variable, near water.
Comments: Feeds on small animals, insects, invertebrates and refuse. Often dunks its food into water before eating it. Most of the human rabies cases in Florida result from raccoon bites.

WEASELS & ALLIES

Members of this group usually have small heads, long necks, short legs and long bodies. All have prominent anal scent glands which are used for social and sexual communication.

STRIPED SKUNK
Mephitis mephitis
Size: To 30 in. (75 cm)
Description: Distinguished by its black coat, white forehead stripe and white side stripes. Predominantly white variants also exist.
Habitat: Open wooded areas, farmland.
Comments: Protects itself by spraying aggressors with noxious smelling fluids from its anal glands. Spray is effective to 15 ft. (5 m) away. Feeds primarily on vegetation, insects and small mammals.

EASTERN SPOTTED SKUNK
Spilogale putorius
Size: To 22 in. (55 cm)
Description: Small black skunk with coat covered with irregular stripes and spots. Tail is white-tipped.
Habitat: Mixed woodlands, wastelands, farmlands.
Comments: When threatened, it gives fair warning by raising its tail, doing a handstand and spreading its hind feet before spraying. A good climber and swimmer, it is more agile than the striped skunk.

NORTHERN RIVER OTTER
Lontra canadensis
Size: To 52 in. (1.3 m)
Description: Torpedo-shaped, glossy brown mammal with short legs, a thick tail and webbed feet.
Habitat: Rivers, ponds, lakes throughout Florida.
Comments: Active during the day, it spends the majority of its time in or near water. Otters are very playful and often build mud slides on riverbanks. Feeds primarily on fish.

MINK
Neovison vison
Size: To 28 in. (70 cm)
Description: Told by rich brown coat, it often has white spotting on chin and throat.
Habitat: Common near water in a variety of habitats.
Comments: Highly aquatic, it dens along river and stream banks and feeds on fish, amphibians, crustaceans and small mammals.

DOG-LIKE MAMMALS

Members of this family have long snouts, large ears and resemble domestic dogs in looks and habit. All are active year-round.

COMMON GRAY FOX
Urocyon cinereoargenteus
Size: To 3.5 ft. (1.1 m)
Description: Distinguished by its coat which is brownish-gray above and rusty-white below.
Habitat: Woodlands, forests.
Comments: Primarily nocturnal, it is occasionally spotted foraging during the day. An excellent climber, it often seeks refuge in trees. The less common red fox (*Vulpes vulpes*) has a white-tipped tail.

COYOTE
Canis latrans
Size: To 52 in. (1.3 m)
Description: Yellow-gray with a pointed nose, rusty legs and ears and a bushy, black-tipped tail.
Habitat: Wooded and open areas.
Comments: Largely a nocturnal hunter, it is often seen loping across fields at dawn and dusk. Holds tail down when running. Feeds on rodents, rabbits, berries and carrion.

CAT-LIKE MAMMALS

This group of highly specialized carnivores are noted for their hunting ability. Most have short faces, keen vision, powerful bodies and retractable claws. Most are nocturnal hunters.

BOBCAT
Lynx rufus
Size: To 4 ft. (1.2 m)
Description: Key field marks are its spotted red-brown coat, short tail and tufted ears.
Habitat: Scrubby open woodlands, thickets, swamps.
Comments: Named for its bobbed tail, it rests in thickets by day and hunts rabbits and rodents by night.

Florida's State Mammal

FLORIDA PANTHER
Puma concolor coryi
Size: To 8 ft. (2.4 m)
Description: Large tan cat with a whitish belly and long, black-tipped tail.
Habitat: Forested habitats.
Comments: A subspecies of mountain lion, it is one of the world's most endangered species. Most of the remaining panthers are closely monitored and a number of programs have been established to enhance their breeding success.

HOOFED MAMMALS

Includes a wide range of hoofed mammals including deer and swine.

WILD BOAR
Sus scrofa
Size: To 6 ft. (1.8 m)
Description: Usually black, pig-like animal has a long grizzled coat and tusks up to 9 in. (23 cm) long. Tail hangs straight and is not coiled.
Habitat: Swamps, brushlands.
Comments: One of the worst invasive species on earth, it devastates large tracts of land by uprooting vegetation and causing excessive erosion. It also devours many native animals including endangered species.

WHITE-TAILED DEER
Odocoileus virginianus
Size: To 7 ft. (2.1 m)
Description: Coat is tan in summer, grayish in winter. Named for its large, white-edged tail which is held aloft, flag-like, when running. Males have prominent antlers which are shed annually from January to March.
Habitat: Forests, farmlands and river valleys.
Comments: An agile, elusive deer, it can reach speeds of 40 mph (65 kph) and leap obstacles as high as 8 ft. (2.5 m). Most active at dawn and dusk. A small, collie-sized subspecies called key deer (O.v. clavium) is found only in the Florida Keys. These unique, endangered deer are easily observed in the National Key Deer Refuge on Big Pine Key.

BEARS

This group includes the largest terrestrial carnivores in the world. All are heavy-bodied, large-headed animals, with short ears and small tails. Their sense of smell is keen, although their eyesight is generally poor.

FLORIDA BLACK BEAR
Ursus americanus floridanus
Size: To 6 ft. (1.8 m)
Description: Large, stout animal has a black, shiny coat, brown nose and stubby tail.
Habitat: Heavily vegetated areas.
Comments: Locally common in a few areas including Ocala National Forest. Diet is predominantly vegetarian, though its also consumes fish, insects, mammals and refuse when readily available. Its distinctive tracks can sometimes be spotted in muddy areas near water. Once considered a threatened species in Florida, it was de-listed in 2012. The population is currently estimated at 3,000.

MARINE MAMMALS

This group includes a variety of mammals that live in the water. The fish-like dolphins and whales spend all their time in the water, breathing atmospheric air through blowholes set high on their heads. Unlike fish, finned marine mammals have horizontal, rather than vertical, tail flukes.

**Florida's State
Marine Mammal**

MANATEE
Trichechus manatus
Size: To 13 ft. (3.9 m)
Description: Large, grayish, walrus-faced aquatic mammal with a broad, paddle-shaped tail.
Habitat: Shallow coastal waters, lagoons, rivers.
Comments: Many believe they were the elusive mermaids that sailors spoke of long ago. Feeds entirely on aquatic vegetation. Florida has more than 20 official marine sanctuaries where these endangered giants can be seen.

BOTTLENOSED DOLPHIN
Tursiops truncatus
Size: To 12 ft. (3.6 m)
Description: Distinguished by its large size, gray color and short beak.
Habitat: Inshore coastal waters, often venturing into freshwater rivers.
Comments: The most common dolphin in Florida waters, it is often found in shallow coastal waters and estuaries Often follows boats or rides on their bow waves.

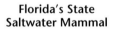

**Florida's State
Saltwater Mammal**

COMMON DOLPHIN
Delphinus delphis
Size: To 9 ft. (2.7 m)
Description: Dark above, white below with yellowish sides and a pronounced snout.
Habitat: Coastal waters, usually offshore.
Comments: Often travels in huge groups and frequently rides the bow waves of ships. Swims at speeds up to 25 mph (40 kph).

SHORT-FINNED PILOT WHALE
Globicephala macrorhynchus
Size: To 23 ft. (7 m)
Description: Dolphin-like whale is black with a bulging forehead.
Habitat: Offshore coastal waters.
Comments: Travels in large groups. Large numbers occasionally beach themselves along the Atlantic coast.

HUMPBACK WHALE
Megaptera novaeangliae
Size: To 53 ft. (16 m)
Description: Dark whale with a humped back and very long flippers with scalloped edges. Underside of flippers and flukes is white.
Habitat: Coastal Atlantic and Gulf waters.
Comments: Frequently observed close to shore during spring and fall migration. Feeds primarily on small schooling fish such as herring.

WHAT ARE BIRDS?

Birds are warm-blooded, feathered animals with two wings and two legs. The majority can fly and those that cannot are believed to be descended from ancestors that did. Adaptations for flight include hollow bones and an enhanced breathing capacity. Birds also have an efficient four-chambered heart and are insulated against the weather to enhance temperature regulation.

HOW TO IDENTIFY BIRDS

As with other species, the best way to become good at identifying birds is simply to practice. The more birds you attempt to identify, the better you will become at distinguishing species.

When birding, the first thing to note is the habitat you are exploring, in order to know what kinds of birds to expect. When you spot a bird, check for obvious field marks. Note the shape of its silhouette and beak. Note the color and pattern of its feathers for distinguishing markings at rest and in flight. Is it small (sparrow), medium (crow), or large (heron)? Does it have any unusual behavioral characteristics?

If you are interested in enhancing your field skills, it is essential to become familiar with bird songs since many species that are difficult to observe in the field are readily identified by their distinctive song. Bird song tapes and CDs are available from nature stores and libraries.

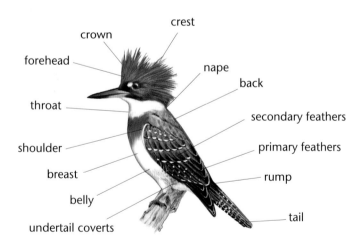

N.B. – *It is important to note that many species illustrations feature the adult male in its breeding coloration. Colors and markings shown may be duller or absent during different times of the year.*

GREBES

The members of this group of duck-like birds have short tails, slender necks and stiff bills. Excellent divers, they have lobed toes rather than webbed feet.

PIED-BILLED GREBE
Podilymbus podiceps
Size: To 13 in. (33 cm)
Description: Small brown bird with a stout, ringed bill and a dark throat.
Habitat: Marshes, ponds.
Comments: Often swims partially submerged.

LARGE WADING BIRDS & SEABIRDS

This general category includes birds from a variety of families. Most inhabit marshes, estuaries and/or coastal waters where they feed on fishes, frogs and insects.

BROWN PELICAN
Pelecanus occidentalis
Size: To 50 in. (1.3 m)
Description: Stout bird with long, pouched beak, light colored head and brownish body.
Habitat: Coastal.
Comments: Common resident feeds by plunging into the water from great heights. The similar American white pelican (*P. erythrorhynchos*) is a winter resident in shallow bays.

Brown

American White

DOUBLE-CRESTED CORMORANT
Phalacrocorax auritus
Size: To 3 ft. (90 cm)
Description: Glossy black bird with a slender neck, hooked bill and orange throat pouch.
Habitat: Common in coastal waters, some found inland.
Comments: Nests in colonies and is often seen perched on trees and pilings near marinas. Often perches with wings outstretched to allow them to dry.

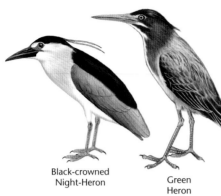

Black-crowned
Night-Heron

Green
Heron

GREEN HERON
Butorides virescens
Size: To 22 in. (55 cm)
Description: Gray-green wading bird has a chestnut neck, a black crown and yellow-orange legs.
Habitat: Ponds, streams, brackish marshes.
Comments: One of a number of herons found stalking fish and frogs in the shallows. Another common Florida heron is the black-and-white black-crowned night-heron (*Nycticorax nycticorax*).

GREAT BLUE HERON
Ardea herodias
Size: To 4.5 ft. (1.4 m)
Description: Large gray-blue bird with long yellow legs, a yellowish, dagger-like bill and whitish face. Note the black plumes extending back from the eye.
Habitat: The borders of rivers, streams and lakes.
Comments: Often seen hunting fish and frogs in still waters. A rare white variant of this species is found in southern Florida.

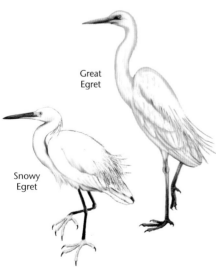

Great
Egret

Snowy
Egret

GREAT EGRET
Ardea alba
Size: To 38 in. (95 cm)
Description: Large white bird with a yellow bill, black legs and black feet.
Habitat: Variable throughout Florida.
Comments: Usually feeds by stalking prey in shallow water and is common along roadsides. The similar snowy egret (*Egretta thula*) is about 12 in. (30 cm) shorter and has a black bill and yellow feet. The stockier, yellow-billed cattle egret (*Bubulcus ibis*: 20 in./50 cm) is the common egret seen feeding in pastures and fields.

WOOD STORK
Mycteria americana
Size: To 4 ft. (1.2 m)
Description: Large, long-legged white bird with a gray, featherless head and neck. Large bill is downturned slightly.
Habitat: Coastal bays, freshwater marshes and ponds.
Comments: An endangered species, it breeds throughout Florida. The largest nesting colony of wood storks is found at the Corkscrew Swamp Sanctuary near Naples.

WHITE IBIS
Eudocimus albus
Size: To 28 in. (70 cm)
Description: Key field marks are white plumage, reddish legs and reddish, downturned bill. Black wing tips are evident in flight.
Habitat: Swamps, marshes, prairies, estuaries.
Comments: Found throughout Florida, they nest, roost and feed in large colonies near lakes and swamps. The glossy ibis (*Plegadis falcinellus*) is also common throughout Florida.

White Ibis

Glossy Ibis

ANHINGA
Anhinga anhinga
Size: To 3 ft. (90 cm)
Description: Large black bird with long, snaking neck, pointed bill and a long tail. Females have a tan neck. Note silvery wing patches.
Habitat: Marshes, swamps, lakes.
Comments: Often perches with wings outspread to let them dry. Slender bill is used to skewer fish while swimming underwater. Also called snakebird, it frequently swims with only its head and bill above water.

ROSEATE SPOONBILL
Ajaia ajaja
Size: To 32 in. (80 cm)
Description: White-pinkish wading bird has unique bill with a flattened, spoon-shaped tip.
Habitat: Mangrove keys, estuaries, mudflats, lagoons.
Comments: It swings its bill from side to side in shallow water while feeding on small fish, crustaceans and insects. It flies with its legs and neck outstretched.

AMERICAN FLAMINGO
Phoenicopterus ruber
Size: To 4 ft. (1.2 m)
Description: Long-legged, long-necked pink bird has a large hooked bill.
Habitat: Salt marshes, mudflats.
Comments: Though symbolic of Florida, most flamingos found here are captive birds from the Caribbean. Wild birds occasionally appear in the south during winter.

SANDHILL CRANE
Grus canadensis
Size: To 4 ft. (1.2 m)
Description: Long-legged gray wading bird has a red forecrown and white cheeks.
Habitat: Freshwater marshes, pastures.
Comments: Unlike herons, it flies with its neck outstretched. Often occurs in large flocks during breeding season.

MAGNIFICENT FRIGATEBIRD
Fregata magnificens
Size: To 40 in. (1 m)
Description: Key field marks are long forked tail, hooked bill and long, narrow angled wings. Male has iridescent black plumage; female is brownish.
Habitat: Coastal waters.
Comments: Has a huge wingspan of up to 8 ft. (2.4 m) wide. Usually roosts and nests in mangrove forests. A threatened species.

LIMPKIN
Aramus guarauna
Size: To 28 in. (70 cm)
Description: Wading bird with
brown plumage streaked with
white and a long, drooping bill.
Habitat: Freshwater marshes.
Comments: When wading, it lifts
its legs high and twitches its tail,
making it appear to limp.

DUCKS & ALLIES

Smaller than geese, ducks have shorter necks and are primarily aquatic.
In most, breeding males are more brightly colored than females. Both sexes
have a brightly colored band (speculum) on the trailing edge of the wing.

BLUE-WINGED TEAL
Anas discors
Size: To 16 in. (40 cm)
Description: Male is distinguished
by its white facial crescent and
white rump.
Habitat: Marshes, ponds, farmlands.
Comments: Florida's most abundant
and widespread winter duck.

WOOD DUCK
Aix sponsa
Size: To 20 in. (50 cm)
Description: Multi-colored, crested
male has a green head, white neck,
red eyes and red bill. Female is
dull-colored with a white eye patch.
Habitat: Wooded ponds, marshes,
lakes, rivers.
Comments: Often seen perching
in trees, it is one of a few ducks to
nest in tree cavities.

MOTTLED DUCK
Anas fulvigula
Size: To 20 in. (50 cm)
Description: Mottled brown duck is
similar to the female mallard but
has a yellower bill and darker tail.
Blue-green speculum lacks a white
border along the leading edge.
Sexes are similar.
Habitat: Marshes, prairies.
Comments: Common year-round
resident is also called the Florida duck.

AMERICAN BLACK DUCK
Anas rubripes
Size: To 25 in. (63 cm)
Description: Sooty, dark duck has a pale brown head and a blue-violet speculum. Wing linings flash white in flight. Sexes are similar.
Habitat: Ponds, marshes, coasts.
Comments: Common in northern Florida and along coasts in winter. Female call is a loud quack; males croak like toads.

RING-NECKED DUCK
Aythya collaris
Size: To 18 in. (45 cm)
Description: Male has ringed bill, dark head and back, and vertical white side stripe. Mottled female is told by similar bill and light eye ring.
Habitat: Wooded lakes, ponds, marshes, open fresh and salt water.
Comments: A wintering duck, it is most common on urban lakes between November and March.

MALLARD
Anas platyrhynchos
Size: To 28 in. (70 cm)
Description: Male has green head, white collar and chestnut breast. The female is mottled brown.
Habitat: Ponds and marshes.
Comments: The ancestor of domestic ducks. Female's call is a loud quack; males do not quack.

GREEN-WINGED TEAL
Anas crecca
Size: To 16 in. (40 cm)
Description: Male has chestnut head and a green eye patch. Female is brown-gray with a green speculum.
Habitat: Lakes and ponds.
Comments: Fast fliers that travel in tight flocks.

RED-BREASTED MERGANSER
Mergus serrator
Size: To 27 in. (68 cm)
Description: Male has a shaggy green head, white neck ring and rusty breast. Females have brownish heads.
Habitat: Coastal, inland lakes and rivers in winter.
Comments: A fish-eating duck, it has a sleek diving profile and a long, slender, toothed bill. Abundant along coasts from October to March.

NORTHERN SHOVELER
Anas clypeata
Size: To 20 in. (50 cm)
Description: Told by its flat head and large, spatulate bill. Male has a green head, rusty sides and a blue wing patch.
Habitat: Fresh and salt water marshes, lakes, ponds.
Comments: Shovel-shaped bill is used to strain aquatic animals and vegetation from the water. Swims with bill pointed downward.

RUDDY DUCK
Oxyura jamaicensis
Size: To 16 in. (40 cm)
Description: Note broad bill and white cheeks. Tail is often cocked in the air when swimming.
Habitat: Lakes, ponds, rivers.
Comments: Common year-round.

AMERICAN COOT
Fulica americana
Size: To 16 in. (40 cm)
Description: A dark bird easily distinguished by its white bill. Legs are long and greenish.
Habitat: Fresh water in the summer and fresh and salt water in winter.
Comments: Feeds on the shore and in the water. Habitually pumps its head back and forth when swimming. Large flocks congregate in shallow marshes during winter.

HAWKS, EAGLES & ALLIES

Primarily carnivorous, these birds have sharp talons for grasping prey, and sharply hooked bills for tearing into flesh. Many soar on wind currents when hunting. Sexes are similar in most.

Turkey Vulture

Black Vulture

TURKEY VULTURE
Cathartes aura
Size: To 32 in. (80 cm)
Description: Large soaring bird with brown-black plumage and a naked red head. Trailing edge of wing feathers are lighter colored giving the bird a two-toned look from below.
Habitat: Dry, open country.
Comments: Feeds on carrion and is often seen along roadsides. Also called a buzzard. The black-headed, black vulture (*Coragyps atratus*) is also common in Florida. Note V-shaped flight profile.

BALD EAGLE
Haliaeetus leucocephalus
Size: To 40 in. (1 m)
Description: Large dark bird with white head and tail, and yellow legs and bill.
Habitat: Near rivers, lakes, ocean.
Comments: Feeds on fish. Florida is home to the largest breeding population of bald eagles in the lower 48 states.

RED-SHOULDERED HAWK
Buteo lineatus
Size: To 22 in. (55 cm)
Description: Brown hawk has rust shoulder patches, brown and white barred wings and a white-banded tail.
Habitat: Deciduous woods, pine scrub, swamps.
Comments: Hunts from a perch for prey including snakes, frogs, rodents and birds.

RED-TAILED HAWK
Buteo jamaicensis
Size: To 25 in. (63 cm)
Description: Large hawk is dark brown above, light below with a red tail. Dark belly band is visible in flight.
Habitat: Open fields and forests.
Comments: Widespread throughout the state, it is often spotted perched on roadside poles and posts.

OSPREY
Pandion haliaetus
Size: To 2 ft. (60 cm)
Description: Large hawk with dark brown back, light underparts and dark eye stripe.
Habitat: Along coast, inland lakes and rivers.
Comments: Unlike most soaring birds, it glides with its wings bent down at the tips. Feeds on fish that it seizes in its talons.

AMERICAN KESTREL
Falco sparverius
Size: To 12 in. (30 cm)
Description: Small falcon with a rust back and tail, and pointed, narrow, spotted blue wings. Males have dark facial marks.
Habitat: Wooded and open areas.
Comments: Formerly called the sparrow hawk. Often pumps tail when perching.

SWALLOW-TAILED KITE
Elanoides forficatus
Size: To 2 ft. (60 cm)
Description: Easily distinguished by its black and white plumage, hooked bill and forked tail.
Habitat: Wooded areas, near lakes and rivers.
Comments: A graceful flier, it spends hours soaring and feeding on the wing. Locally common in a few areas including Clewiston.

CRESTED CARACARA
Caracara cheriway
Size: To 25 in. (63 cm)
Description: Key field marks are black head crest, red face and long legs.
Habitat: Open woodlands, prairies in central Florida.
Comments: Often seen running along the ground in search of prey. It also eats carrion and is dominant over vultures at kills.

CHICKEN-LIKE BIRDS

These ground-dwelling birds are chicken-like in both looks and habits. Most have stout bills, rounded wings and heavy bodies. Primarily terrestrial, they are capable of short bursts of flight.

WILD TURKEY
Meleagris gallopavo
Size: To 4 ft. (1.2 m)
Description: Resembles a slim domestic turkey. Males have blue to pink facial patches and red fleshy wattles under the bill.
Habitat: Open woodlands, hammocks, prairies.
Comments: Males are often heard 'gobbling' at dawn as they gather the females in their flock. Most roost in trees at night.

NORTHERN BOBWHITE
Colinus virginianus
Size: To 12 in. (30 cm)
Description: A small, plump brown bird with a small head and short tail. Males have a white throat and eye stripe.
Habitat: Open woodlands, roadsides, wood edges, brushy fields.
Comments: This ground dweller is often flushed by hikers. Call is a clear – *bob-WHITE!*

SHOREBIRDS & ALLIES

This general category includes wading birds normally found along shorelines. Most are brownish and have slender bills which they use to probe the sand and mud for invertebrates.

SANDERLING
Calidris alba
Size: To 8 in. (20 cm)
Description: Light gray above, white below with black legs and a black bill.
Habitat: Seashores, mudflats.
Comments: Very common from August to March. They often run in and out with the surf, probing their bills in the wet sand in search of invertebrates.

Winter Plumage

BLACK-BELLIED PLOVER
Pluvialis squatarola
Size: To 14 in. (35 cm)
Description: Large, stocky shorebird is mottled above, light below with a black beak and legs.
Habitat: Mudflats and coastal shores.
Comments: Feeds by tilting forward, taking a few steps, and tilting forward again. Spends summers in the Arctic.

RUDDY TURNSTONE
Arenaria interpres
Size: To 10 in. (25 cm)
Description: Squat brownish bird with black bib and orange legs. Belly and rump are white.
Habitat: Mudflats and coastal shores.
Comments: Uses its strong bill to turn over shells and other objects when searching for food. Most abundant in winter.

KILLDEER
Charadrius vociferus
Size: To 12 in. (30 cm)
Description: Thick-necked, short-billed bird with a brown back, white breast and two black breast bands. Rump shows orange in flight.
Habitat: Seashore, fields, pastures, parks, open areas.
Comments: Shrill call – *kill-dee, kill-dee* – is repeated continuously.

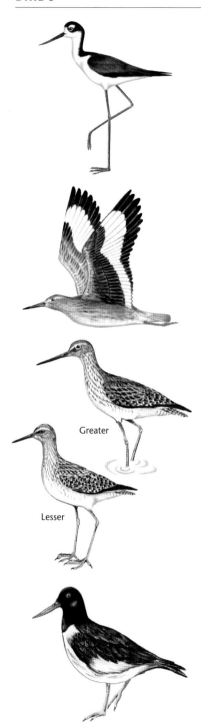

Greater

Lesser

BLACK-NECKED STILT
Himantopus mexicanus
Size: To 17 in. (43 cm)
Description: Easily distinguished by its black and white plumage and long, thin legs, neck and bill.
Habitat: Shorelines of fresh and salt water habitats.
Comments: Call is a repetitive series of piping notes.

WILLET
Tringa semipalmata
Size: To 17 in. (43 cm)
Description: Long-legged, long-billed gray shorebird. Wings flash black and white in flight.
Habitat: Shorelines, mudflats.
Comments: Noisy birds, their call sounds like a loud – *pill-will-willet* – or a softer – *kuk-kuk-kuk.*

GREATER YELLOWLEGS
Tringa melanoleuca
Size: To 15 in. (38 cm)

LESSER YELLOWLEGS
Tringa flavipes
Size: To 10 in. (25 cm)
Description: Distinguished from other shorebirds by their large size and long, bright yellow legs. The greater yellowlegs is taller and has a thicker bill that may be upturned slightly.
Habitat: Coastal wetlands, lake and pond margins.
Comments: The calls of the two species are distinctive; the greater has a descending three- to four-note call – *kyew, kyew, kyew* – while the lesser's is one- or two-notes – *tu, tu.*

AMERICAN OYSTERCATCHER
Haematopus palliatus
Size: To 20 in. (50 cm)
Description: Distinguished by brown back, white underparts, black head and stout orange bill.
Habitat: Shorelines, mudflats.
Comments: Feeds primarily on shellfish. Call is a shrill – *kleeep.*

AMERICAN AVOCET
Recurvirostra americana
Size: To 20 in. (50 cm)
Description: Large shorebird with long legs and a long upcurved bill. Breeding birds have a tawny head and neck.
Habitat: Shallow ponds, marshes, mudflats.
Comments: Feeds by working bill side to side while walking through the water.

GULLS & ALLIES

These long-winged birds are strong fliers and excellent swimmers. Gulls are usually gray and white and have webbed feet and square tails; immature birds are brownish. Terns are smaller with narrow wings, forked tails and pointed bills.

LAUGHING GULL
Leucophaeus atricilla
Size: To 18 in. (45 cm)
Description: Small coastal gull has a dark gray mantle and black wing tips. Head is black in summer, white with a dark smudge in winter.
Habitat: Marshes, bays, beaches, piers.
Comments: A year-round resident of Florida. Call resembles a loud laugh – *ha-ha-ha.*

RING-BILLED GULL
Larus delawarensis
Size: To 20 in. (50 cm)
Description: Key field marks are a black-ringed bill, yellow eyes, yellow legs and a dark-tipped white tail.
Habitat: Found near lakes, rivers, fields, dumps and shopping malls.
Comments: Varied diet includes carrion, garbage, eggs, young birds and aquatic animals. The similar herring gull (*L. argentatus*) has pink legs and a red bill spot.

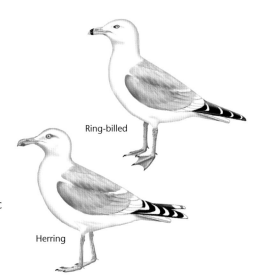

Ring-billed

Herring

ROYAL TERN
Thalasseus maximus
Size: To 22 in. (55 cm)
Description: Large tern has light gray primaries, a slightly crested head and a bright orange bill. Crown is black in summer. Tail is forked.
Habitat: Coastal.
Comments: Common on both coasts year-round. Feeds by plunging into the ocean after fish. One of several similar species of tern occurring in Florida.

BLACK SKIMMER
Rynchops niger
Size: To 20 in. (50 cm)
Description: Distinguished by black and white plumage, long wings and long, black-tipped, orange bill. The lower bill is longer than the upper.
Habitat: Coastal, inland lakes.
Comments: Skimmer feeds by flying with its lower bill cutting water; when it feels a fish, the upper bill snaps down. They often fly in flocks. Call resembles a dog's bark.

DOVES

These familiar birds are common and widespread. All species coo. They feed largely on seeds, grain and insects.

Mourning

Eurasian

MOURNING DOVE
Zenaida macroura
Size: To 13 in. (33 cm)
Description: Slender tawny bird with a relatively long neck, small head and a long, pointed tail.
Habitat: Open woodlands, suburbs.
Comments: Named for its mournful, cooing song; most frequently heard in the early morning. It feeds on the ground in flocks and bobs its head back and forth when walking. Its wings whistle loudly in flight. One of a few Florida game birds. The similar Eurasian collared dove (*Streptopelia decaocto*) has a dark band on its nape.

ROCK PIGEON
Columba livia
Size: To 13 in. (33 cm)
Description: The familiar bird is typically blue-gray, though white, tan and brown variants also exist. Rump is white.
Habitat: Common in cities, towns and farmlands.
Comments: This introduced species is both gregarious and tame and can be trained for homing.

OWLS

These square-shaped birds of prey have large heads, large eyes and hooked bills. Large flattened areas around each eye form 'facial disks' which help to amplify sound toward external ear flaps. Primarily nocturnal. Sexes are similar.

BURROWING OWL
Athene cunicularia
Size: To 11 in. (28 cm)
Description: Small terrestrial owl is told at a glance by its long legs and yellow eyes.
Habitat: Grassy fields, open plains, dry pastures, airports.
Comments: Locally common on prairies of central Florida. They live underground in burrows and often nest in small colonies. The other small Florida owl, the eastern screech owl (*Megascops asio*) has yellow eyes and prominent ear tufts.

Burrowing   Eastern Screech

GREAT HORNED OWL
Bubo virginianus
Size: To 25 in. (63 cm)
Description: Large, dark brown bird with prominent ear tufts, yellow eyes and a white throat.
Habitat: Wooded areas.
Comments: Primarily nocturnal, it feeds on small mammals and birds. Sometimes spotted hunting during the day. Voice is a deep, resonant – *hoo-HOO-hoooo*.

CUCKOOS & ALLIES

Slender birds have rounded wings and a curved beak.

YELLOW-BILLED CUCKOO
Coccyzus americanus
Size: To 14 in. (35 cm)
Description: Plumage is brown above and white below. Narrow tail is distinctively striped on the underside.
Habitat: Forests, gardens.
Comments: Call is a repetitive – *ka-ka-ka-koup-koup-koup.*

GOATSUCKERS

These nocturnal insect-eaters have large, swallow-like heads. Ancients believed that the birds sucked the milk of goats with their gaping mouths.

COMMON NIGHTHAWK
Chordeiles minor
Size: To 10 in. (25 cm)
Description: Gray-brown bird with a large head, short bill and white throat. Long, pointed wings have prominent white bars that are evident in flight.
Habitat: Forests, open country, cities.
Comments: Spectacular fliers, they can often be seen hawking for insects at dusk and dawn near street lights.

HUMMINGBIRDS

The smallest birds, hummingbirds are named for the noise made by their wings during flight. All have long needle-like bills and extensible tongues which are used to extract nectar from flowers.

RUBY-THROATED HUMMINGBIRD
Archilochus colubris
Size: To 3.5 in. (9 cm)
Description: Plumage is green above, whitish below. Only male has a bright red throat.
Habitat: Forests, cities.
Comments: Often found hovering in meadows and gardens near flowers. When defending their territory, males will often swoop down to 'buzz' intruders.

KINGFISHERS

Solitary, broad-billed birds renowned for their fishing expertise.

BELTED KINGFISHER
Megaceryle alcyon
Size: To 14 in. (35 cm)
Description: Stocky blue-gray bird with a large crested head and a long, stout bill.
Habitat: Near clear water.
Comments: Often seen perched on powerlines or in trees near water. Usually hovers over water before plunging in after fish.

WOODPECKERS

These strong-billed birds are usually spotted on tree trunks chipping away bark in search of insects. All have stiff tails that serve as props as they forage. In spring, males drum on dead limbs and other resonant objects (e.g., garbage cans, drainpipes) to establish their territories.

RED-BELLIED WOODPECKER
Melanerpes carolinus
Size: To 11 in. (28 cm)
Description: Robin-sized woodpecker with a black and white striped back. Male has a red cap and nape; female has a red nape only. Reddish belly patch is seldom visible.
Habitat: Deciduous and mixed woods, backyards.
Comments: Very common and widespread throughout Florida. The red-headed woodpecker (*M. erythrocephalus*) has a head that is all red.

Red-headed

Red-bellied

NORTHERN FLICKER
Colaptes auratus
Size: To 13 in. (33 cm)
Description: Brown, jay-sized bird with barred back, spotted breast and black bib. Wing and tail linings are yellow. Male has black mustache.
Habitat: Woodlands, open areas, suburbs.
Comments: Commonly forages on the ground in search of insects and invertebrates.

Hairy

Downy

DOWNY WOODPECKER
Picoides pubescens
Size: To 6 in. (15 cm)
Description: A small, sparrow-sized, black and white woodpecker with a small bill. Males have a small red head patch.
Habitat: Wooded areas.
Comments: Common resident is often seen at feeders in winter. The similar, hairy woodpecker (*Picoides villosus*; 10 in./25 cm) is larger and has a longer bill.

PILEATED WOODPECKER
Dryocopus pileatus
Size: To 17 in. (43 cm)
Description: Large black bird distinguished by its prominent red head crest and white neck stripes. Large white wing patches are evident in flight.
Habitat: Forests.
Comments: A wary bird, it can be detected by the slow, rhythmic hammering noise it makes excavating cavities in trees while foraging for insects.

FLYCATCHERS

These compact birds characteristically sit on exposed perches and dart out to capture passing insects and return to the same perch. Many species have hairy bristles at the base of their bills.

GREAT CRESTED FLYCATCHER
Myiarchus crinitus
Size: To 9 in. (23 cm)
Description: Robin-sized bird is distinguished by its yellow belly, gray breast and rust wings and tail.
Habitat: Woodlands.
Comments: Often glides between trees with wings outspread. Breeds throughout Florida and often over-winters in the southern part of the state.

EASTERN KINGBIRD
Tyrannus tyrannus
Size: To 8 in. (20 cm)
Description: Distinguished by its dark back, black mask, white under-parts and white band on tip of tail.
Habitat: Open woodlands and shrubby meadows.
Comments: This aggressive, noisy bird is highly territorial and will defend its nesting areas against all intruders, including people. A similar flycatcher, the eastern phoebe (*Sayornis phoebe*) lacks a tail band.

Kingbird

Phoebe

SWALLOWS

These streamlined, acrobatic fliers have short legs, short bills, long pointed wings and long tails (often forked). Their wide mouths are adapted for scooping up insects on the wing.

PURPLE MARTIN
Progne subis
Size: To 8 in. (20 cm)
Description: Distinguished by its purple-black plumage and slightly forked tail.
Habitat: Wooded areas in cities and towns.
Comments: Frequently glides in circles when flying. Nests in colonies, and is easily attracted to multi-celled bird houses. Most common between January and July.

TREE SWALLOW
Tachycineta bicolor
Size: To 6 in. (15 cm)
Description: Plumage is glossy blue-green above and white below. Females are brownish above and white below.
Habitat: Wooded areas near water.
Comments: Huge flocks numbering in the thousands arrive in winter to feed on wild fruit.

JAYS, CROWS ETC.

These large, omnivorous birds are very common. Most have stout bills with bristles near the base. Sexes are similar.

BLUE JAY
Cyanocitta cristata
Size: To 14 in. (35 cm)
Description: Easily recognized by its crested head, blue back, and black neckband.
Habitat: Woodlands and open areas.
Comments: Widespread throughout Florida, they are bold, aggressive birds that often dominate backyard feeders. They have several vocalizations, some of which are quite musical. Call is a loud – *jay-jay-jay!*

FLORIDA SCRUB JAY
Aphelocoma coerulescens
Size: To 13 in. (33 cm)
Description: A streamlined blue bird with a long bill and tail. Key field marks are white throat, incomplete blue necklace and brown back.
Habitat: Scrub and oak habitats.
Comments: Locally common in a few locations in Florida, its numbers have declined in recent years due to habitat loss.

AMERICAN CROW
Corvus brachyrhynchos
Size: To 22 in. (55 cm)
Description: Told by black plumage and thick black bill. Call is a distinct – *caw.*
Habitat: Rural and wilderness areas.
Comments: Eats everything from insects and grain to small birds and refuse. The similar, slightly smaller, fish crow (*C. ossifragus;* 20 in./50 cm) is more common in coastal and urban areas. Its call is a nasal – *uh, uh.*

CHICKADEES & ALLIES

Small, friendly birds with short bills and long tails that occur in small flocks.

CAROLINA CHICKADEE
Poecile carolinensis
Size: To 4.5 in. (11 cm)
Description: Identified by its small size, fluffy gray plumage, black cap and bib and white face patch.
Habitat: Deciduous woods, urban areas.
Comments: Very active and inquisitive, they are easily attracted to feeders and tame enough to be fed by hand. Name-saying call is a clear – *chickadee-dee-dee-dee.*

TUFTED TITMOUSE
Baeolophus bicolor
Size: To 6 in. (15 cm)
Description: Gray above, light below with reddish flanks and a prominent crest.
Habitat: Moist deciduous woodlands, city parks.
Comments: Highly social birds, they are common at feeders in winter. Call sounds like – *peter, peter.*

WRENS

These little brown birds have the distinctive habit of cocking their tails in the air. They spend much of their time on the ground and in low bushes foraging for insects.

CAROLINA WREN
Thyrothorus ludovicianus
Size: To 6 in. (15 cm)
Description: Brown above, buff colored below with a white throat and white eye stripe.
Habitat: Thickets, brushy areas, ravines, towns.
Comments: One of the most common and widespread Florida birds. Often nests in man-made containers including flower pots and old hats. Call is a loud, whistled – *teakettle-teakettle-teakettle.*

MOCKINGBIRDS & ALLIES

Long-tailed, slender-billed birds with decurved bills that sing loudly from exposed perches.

NORTHERN MOCKINGBIRD
Mimus polyglottos
Size: To 11 in. (28 cm)
Description: Slender, long-tailed bird with gray back and light underparts. Wings flash white in flight.
Habitat: Woodlands, urban parks and gardens.
Comments: A superb singer that is named for its habit of mimicking ambient sounds ranging from the calls of other birds to traffic noises.

Florida's State Bird

BROWN THRASHER
Toxostoma rufum
Size: To 12 in. (30 cm)
Description: Rich brown above and heavily streaked below, it is distinguished by its long tail and slightly decurved bill.
Habitat: Edges of woodlands and thickets, city parks, farmlands.
Comments: Imitates sounds like the mockingbird but repeats phrases once, rather than continuously. Most common in central and northern Florida, it often forages in yards.

THRUSHES

This group of woodland birds includes many good singers. Most feed on the ground. Sexes are similar.

EASTERN BLUEBIRD
Sialia sialis
Size: To 7 in. (18 cm)
Description: Brilliant blue bird with an orange breast and a white belly. Females are duller with a grayish head.
Habitat: Open woodlands, fields.
Comments: Song is a liquid-like melodious warble.

AMERICAN ROBIN
Turdus migratorius
Size: To 11 in. (28 cm)
Description: Familiar to most, it is told by its gray back and rust breast.
Habitat: Very common in towns, fields and open woodlands.
Comments: Forages on the ground for insects, snails and worms. Most abundant in spring and fall. Song is a melodious series of rising and falling notes – *cheer-up, cheerily, cheer-up, cheery.*

WAXWINGS

These gregarious birds are named for their red wing marks that look like waxy droplets.

CEDAR WAXWING
Bombycilla cedrorum
Size: To 7 in. (18 cm)
Description: Told at a glance by its sleek, crested head and yellow-tipped tail. Note red, waxy wing spots.
Habitat: Open woods, orchards.
Comments: A common winter bird found in large flocks throughout Florida from November to March.

STARLINGS

Introduced from Europe, they are abundant in cities and towns.

EUROPEAN STARLING
Sturnus vulgaris
Size: To 8 in. (20 cm)
Description: Chubby bird with a yellow bill and a short tail. In winter, the plumage becomes brightly flecked and the bill darkens.
Habitat: Fields, cities.
Comments: Considered a pest by many, it outcompetes many native species for food and nesting sights. Usually travels in huge flocks.

WARBLERS & ALLIES

Members of this large family of highly active, insect-eating birds are distinguished from other small birds by their thin, pointed bills. Males tend to be more brightly colored than females and are the only singers. Those that are migrants tend to be duller-colored than shown here.

COMMON YELLOWTHROAT
Geothlypis trichas
Size: To 5 in. (13 cm)
Description: Olive green above, yellow below with a white-bordered black mask. Females are dull yellow below and lack the mask.
Habitat: Moist, grassy areas, marshes, thickets.
Comments: A year-round resident, it is abundant and widespread throughout the state.

Palm

PALM WARBLER
Setophaga palmarum
Size: To 6 in. (15 cm)
Description: Plumage is typically olive-brown above and yellowish below. Note breast streaking. Rust cap is key field mark in spring.
Habitat: Hammocks, beaches, lawns and prairies.
Comments: One of the most common warblers in southern Florida during winter, it often wags or bobs its tail while perching. The pine warbler (*S. pinus*) is also common throughout Florida.

Pine

YELLOW-RUMPED WARBLER
Setophaga coronata
Size: To 6 in. (15 cm)
Description: Key field marks are yellow rump, yellow cap and white throat. The rarely seen western race of this species has a yellow throat.
Habitat: Mixed forests.
Comments: Formerly considered two separate species, the myrtle and Audubon's warblers. Most common during spring and fall migrations when its plumage is drab brown.

'Myrtle' race

BLACKBIRDS & ALLIES

A diverse group of birds ranging from iridescent black birds to brightly colored meadowlarks and orioles. All have conical, sharp-pointed bills.

COMMON GRACKLE
Quiscalus quiscula
Size: To 14 in. (35 cm)
Description: Black-purple bird with long, wedge-shaped tail and yellow eyes.
Habitat: Open woods, fields, parks, lawns.
Comments: Common resident that occurs in large flocks during winter. Abundant near human dwellings. The similar, larger, boat-tailed grackle (*Q. major*) is more common in coastal areas.

Common

Boat-tailed

RED-WINGED BLACKBIRD
Agelaius phoeniceus
Size: To 9 in. (23 cm)
Description: Black male has distinctive red shoulder patches. Brown females look like large sparrows.
Habitat: Swamps, marshes and wet fields.
Comments: Usually nests in reeds or tall grass near water and is common in urban parks. Gurgling, musical song is a common marsh sound.

BALTIMORE ORIOLE
Icterus galbula
Size: To 8 in. (20 cm)
Description: Distinctive black and orange bird has a full black hood.
Habitat: Open deciduous forests.
Comments: Builds a distinctive hanging nest in deciduous trees. Common throughout Florida. The similar orchard oriole (*I. spurius*) occurs in the northern half of Florida. It has chestnut plumage and a dark hood and back.

Baltimore

Orchard

EASTERN MEADOWLARK
Sturnella magna
Size: To 9 in. (23 cm)
Description: Mottled brown bird with a bright yellow breast, white-edged tail, and dark V-shaped neckband.
Habitat: Grassy fields, meadows, marshes.
Comments: Nests and forages on the ground. Loud, flute-like, gurgling song is distinctive.

FINCHES, SPARROWS & ALLIES

Members of this family have short, thick, seed-cracking bills.

NORTHERN CARDINAL
Cardinalis cardinalis
Size: To 9 in. (23 cm)
Description: Bright, red crested bird with a black mask and a stout bill.
Habitat: Woodlands, gardens, parks, backyards.
Comments: Very common in cities and towns throughout the year. Easily attracted to feeders in winter.

CHIPPING SPARROW
Spizella passerina
Size: To 5 in. (13 cm)
Description: Brown bird with a rust cap, white eyebrow line, black line through eye and unstreaked breast.
Habitat: Open forests, fields, lawns, gardens.
Comments: Call is a series of sharp, repetitive chips.

AMERICAN GOLDFINCH
Spinus tristis
Size: To 5 in. (13 cm)
Description: Male is bright yellow with a black cap, black tail and wings and a white rump. Duller female lacks a cap.
Habitat: Wooded groves, gardens.
Comments: Often found in flocks. Can be identified on the wing by its deeply undulating flight. Canary-like song is bright and cheery.

EASTERN TOWHEE
Pipilo erythrophthalmus
Size: To 9 in. (23 cm)
Description: Told by its dark hood and back, rusty sides, and white belly. Female is brown where the male is black. Eyes may be red or white.
Habitat: Woodlands and brushy areas, lawns.
Comments: The white- and red-eyed races represent two distinct subspecies. Song is a buzzy – *drink-your-teeeaaaa,* or – *towweeeeeee.*

INDIGO BUNTING
Passerina cyanea
Size: To 6 in. (15 cm)
Description: Brilliant blue bird is unmistakable. Females are brownish.
Habitat: Woodlands, fields.
Comments: Males sing from exposed perches in summer. The equally brilliant painted bunting (*P. ciris*) is also common in Florida.

Indigo

Painted

WEAVER FINCHES

These sparrow-like birds were introduced to North America in 1850, and are now widespread throughout the continent.

HOUSE SPARROW
Passer domesticus
Size: To 6 in. (15 cm)
Description: Black throat and brown nape of male are diagnostic. Females and young are dull brown with a light eye stripe.
Habitat: Very common in a variety of habitats.
Comments: Introduced from Europe, these gregarious, social birds are common throughout Florida.

WHAT ARE REPTILES & AMPHIBIANS?

Reptiles and amphibians represent a diverse array of water- and land-dwelling animals.

REPTILES

Reptiles can generally be described as scaly-skinned, terrestrial creatures that breathe through lungs. The majority reproduce by laying eggs on land; in some, the eggs develop inside the mother who later gives birth to live young. Contrary to popular belief, very few are harmful to man. All are valuable in controlling rodent and insect populations.

The most common types of Florida reptiles are turtles, lizards and snakes.

AMPHIBIANS

Amphibians are smooth-skinned, limbed vertebrates that live in moist habitats and breathe through either lungs, skin, gills or a combination of all three. While they spend much of their lives on land, they still depend on a watery environment to complete their life cycle. Most reproduce by laying eggs in or near water. The young hatch as swimming larvae – tadpoles, for example – which breathe through gills. After a short developmental period, the larvae metamorphose into young adults with lungs and legs.

The most common types of Florida amphibians are salamanders, frogs and toads.

HOW TO IDENTIFY REPTILES & AMPHIBIANS

Reptiles are secretive but can be observed if you know where to look. Turtles are found on the edges of ponds and lakes and often sun themselves on rocks and logs. Lizards sun themselves in habitats ranging from open deserts to suburban back yards and are the most conspicuous reptiles. The best time to look for snakes is in the early morning or late afternoon when it's not too hot. They can be found in deserts, canyons and along trails and watercourses. Look in meadows, fields, woods, or on the margins of ponds, checking under sun-warmed logs and rocks where they may be resting.

Of the amphibians, frogs and toads are probably the easiest to observe since they loudly announce their presence during breeding season. Frogs are found in wet areas on or near the water. Toads are more terrestrial and may be found far from water, especially during the day. Salamanders are more secretive and rarely venture out of their cool, moist habitats.

Caution – When seeking reptiles, watch where you step. Many snakes are well-camouflaged and can be sluggish in the morning or after eating. Also, be careful where you put your hands. Do not put hands in places you can't see into. Turn over rocks and logs with a stick or tool.

CROCODILIANS

Crocodilians are large reptiles that have armor-plated skin and huge, toothy jaws. All are aquatic carnivores that feed on fish and other animals. Only the alligator and crocodile are native to North America. All are dangerous to humans. Three species are found in Florida.

AMERICAN ALLIGATOR
Alligator mississippiensis
Size: To 19 ft. (5.7 m)
Description: Distinguished by broad, rounded snout and blackish color. When jaws are closed, only upper teeth are visible.
Habitat: Freshwater lakes, bayous, marshes and swamps.
Comments: During droughts, the alligator excavates a pool (gator hole) in marshes which is beneficial to many forms of wildlife. During cooler months, it hibernates in dens along the banks of waterways and lakes.

Florida's State Reptile

AMERICAN CROCODILE
Crocodylus acutus
Size: To 15 ft. (4.5 m)
Description: It is distinguished from the alligator by its gray-green color and slender, tapering snout. Large fourth tooth on bottom jaw is visible when mouth is closed.
Habitat: Saltwater shorelines and brackish swamps in extreme SE Florida.
Comments: An endangered species, only about 500 remain in the wild. Typically much more aggressive than the alligator. It is found in coastal southern Florida and the Keys.

SPECTACLED CAIMAN
Caiman crocodilus
Size: To 8 ft. (2.4 m)
Description: Greenish to brown in color with light crossbanding down its back. There is a curved bony ridge in front of its eyes.
Habitat: Ponds, marshes, rivers.
Comments: Imported for the pet trade from South America, many escaped or were released and survive today in drainage canals and rivers in extreme southern Florida.

TURTLES

Turtles are easily distinguished by their large bony carapaces (shells). The shell is formed from widened ribs and protects the turtle from most predators. Like all reptiles, turtles breathe air through lungs; they are also able to breathe underwater from gill-like respiratory surfaces on the mouth and anus. Turtles are most active in spring during mating season. Females lay eggs in holes excavated in sand or soft soil near water. The young hatch either in late summer or the following spring and are independent from birth. Most eat a wide variety of plant and animal matter. There are 32 species of turtles found in Florida.

FLORIDA REDBELLY COOTER
Pseudemys nelsoni
Size: To 15 in. (38 cm)
Description: Highly arched, blackish carapace has red markings often hidden beneath algae and mosses. Underbelly (plaston) is red to orange. Note yellow stripes on head and arrow-shaped stripe between eyes.
Habitat: Lakes, streams, ponds, mangrove swamps.
Comments: Often basks in the company of other turtles. Feeds primarily on aquatic plants.

FLORIDA SOFTSHELL
Apalone ferox
Size: To 25 in. (63 cm)
Description: Brownish turtle distinguished by its flat, leathery shell, tubular snout and striped head.
Habitat: Lakes, ponds and slow rivers with sandy or muddy bottoms.
Comments: Often swims submerged, breathing snorkel-like through its snout.

GOPHER TORTOISE
Gopherus polyphemus
Size: To 14 in. (35 cm)
Description: Told at a glance by its domed, ridged shell and elephantine hind limbs.
Habitat: Sandy areas, often far from water.
Comments: Strictly terrestrial, it digs long burrows in sandy soils. These burrows are used for shelter by hundreds of other animals including raccoons, opossums, burrowing owls, gopher frogs, snakes and insects. It feeds primarily on vegetation.

PENINSULAR COOTER
Pseudemys peninsularis
Size: To 16 in. (40 cm)
Description: Brown shell is covered with a network of yellow markings. Key field marks are numerous yellow head and neck markings, some of which form hairpin shapes on the back of the head.
Habitat: Ponds, lakes, swamps, marshes, rivers.
Comments: One of Florida's most common turtles, it is often seen basking on banks and logs or crossing roadways.

FLORIDA SNAPPING TURTLE
Chelydra serpentina osceola
Size: To 18 in. (45 cm)
Description: Distinguished by its rough, knobby shell and long tail that is saw-toothed on its upper edge.
Habitat: Ponds and lakes with muddy bottoms and abundant vegetation.
Comments: An aggressive predator, it feeds on fishes, amphibians, reptiles, mammals and birds. It should be treated with caution when encountered on land as it will often lunge at humans and can inflict serious cuts. Its massive cousin, the alligator snapping turtle (*Macroclemys temmincki*), found in northern Florida, weighs up to 200 lbs. (90 kg).

Florida Snapping Turtle

Alligator Snapping Turtle

RED-EARED SLIDER
Trachemys scripta elegans
Size: To 11 in. (28 cm)
Description: Distinguished by its round, yellow-marked shell and red ear patch.
Habitat: Ponds, quiet streams, marshes, ditches.
Comments: The common pet store turtle. Many have been introduced to the wild by their owners and may outnumber native turtles in some areas.

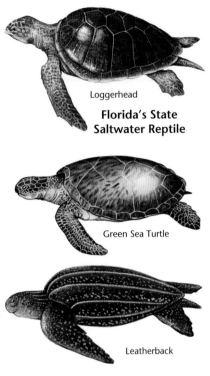

Loggerhead

Florida's State Saltwater Reptile

Green Sea Turtle

Leatherback

LOGGERHEAD SEA TURTLE
Caretta caretta
Size: To 4 ft. (1.2 m)
Description: Huge red-brown turtle with elongate, heart-shaped carapace, large, blunt head and paddle-like limbs.
Habitat: Open ocean and coastal bays and streams.
Comments: Nests twice or more a year on sandy beaches along both coasts. After mating, the female drags herself above the high water line, excavates a nest cavity, and lays her eggs. The young are independent from birth and must fend for themselves. The endangered loggerhead is the most common of the five marine turtles that visit Florida. Loggerheads, green sea turtles (*Chelonia mydas*) and leatherbacks (*Dermochelys coriacea*) all nest in Florida; the most popular nesting area is between Cape Canaveral and Palm Beach.

LIZARDS

Lizards are scaly-skinned animals which usually have moveable eyelids, visible ear openings, claws and toothed jaws. There are 61 species found in Florida.

Green

Cuban Brown

GREEN ANOLE
Anolis carolinensis
Size: To 8 in. (20 cm)
Description: Slender green lizard with a long, wedge-shaped snout and a pink or gray throat fan (dewlap). Able to change color from green to brown to match backgrounds of leaves or bark.
Habitat: Variable, including forests, swamps and urban areas throughout Florida.
Comments: Diurnal and often encountered on walls, tree limbs and fence posts. One of at least six anoles now found in Florida. The similar, introduced Cuban brown anole (*A. sagrei*) is also very common.

EASTERN FENCE LIZARD
Sceloporus undulatus undulatus
Size: To 8 in. (20 cm)
Description: Female and juvenile have black and white zigzag bars on their backs. Adult male has bluish patches on its throat and flanks.
Habitat: Deciduous and coniferous woods, sandy areas, urban gardens.
Comments: Active during the day, it spends most of its time on fences and other man-made structures.

MEDITERRANEAN GECKO
Hemidactylus turcicus
Size: To 5 in. (13 cm)
Description: Flattened, short-limbed pinkish-brown lizard has large eyes and pimply, blotched skin. Spots on body may be brown, gray, pinkish or ivory. It lacks eyelids and has enlarged toe pads and unwebbed feet.
Habitat: Urban areas, usually on or near buildings.
Comments: An introduced species, it is active in the evenings foraging for insects and is often spotted on buildings or near insect-attracting lights.

SOUTHEASTERN FIVE-LINED SKINK
Plestiodon inexpectatus
Size: To 9 in. (23 cm)
Description: Brown, cylindrical lizard has smooth, glossy scales and five light dorsal stripes edged in black. The tails of young skinks are bright blue.
Habitat: Woodlands and forests beneath leaf litter.
Comments: Active during the day, it often suns itself on logs or stumps. Like many lizards, its tail readily detaches when grasped by a predator; in such instances the detached tail wriggles, providing a diversion which often allows the skink to escape. The tail grows back in a few weeks.

SNAKES

Snakes are limbless reptiles with moist, scaly skin, toothed jaws, no ear openings or eyelids and a single row of belly scales. They move by contracting their muscles in waves and undulating over the ground. All are carnivorous and swallow their prey whole. They flick their tongues in and out constantly to 'taste' and 'smell' the air around them. Most continue to grow in length during their life and shed their outer skin periodically. The vast majority are harmless to man. There are 75 species found in Florida, only six of which are venomous.

NON-VENOMOUS SNAKES

SOUTHERN BLACK RACER

Coluber constrictor priapus
Size: To 6 ft. (1.8 m)
Description: Usually a dull black or slate gray snake with a white chin and throat.
Habitat: Variable, though usually near water.
Comments: Active during the day, racers thrive in cities and are probably the most frequently observed Florida snake. Feeds primarily on mice and other small rodents. Often seen crossing roads. Holds its head and neck high when foraging and is fast-moving.

EASTERN HOGNOSE SNAKE

Heterodon platirhinos
Size: To 4 ft. (1.2 m)
Description: Thick-necked snake has an upturned snout. Color varies considerably, ranging from black and brown to yellow.
Habitat: Sandy areas, open woodlands, hillsides and fields.

Comments: Uses its upturned snout as a shovel to excavate its favorite prey, the spadefoot toad. Though harmless, it fakes an aggressive display when disturbed by puffing itself up, hissing loudly and striking out, though it rarely bites. If this tactic fails to deter predators, it will play dead and excrete a foul-smelling musk.

EASTERN CORN SNAKE
Pantherophis guttatus
Size: To 6 ft. (1.8 m)
Description: Beautiful red-orange to brown snake with black-bordered reddish blotches down back. Color can vary considerably, with gray and yellow phases also found in Florida.
Habitat: Woods, farmlands, roadsides, prairies, cities.
Comments: One of the state's most conspicuous snakes, it is an expert rodent catcher that is often bred in captivity. A good climber, it readily ascends trees. Also called red rat snake.

SOUTHERN RINGNECK SNAKE
Diadophis punctatus punctatus
Size: To 18 in. (45 cm)
Description: A slender brown to black snake with a neck ring and yellowish, black-spotted belly scales. Neck ring is often interrupted.
Habitat: Near water in swamps, prairies, forests and meadows, throughout Florida.
Comments: This very common snake is often found near homes where it feeds on snails, slugs and amphibians. When threatened, it will tightly coil its tail and expose its brightly colored, spotted belly scales.

BURMESE PYTHON
Python molurus bivattatus
Size: To 16.5 ft. (5 m)
Description: Very large, thick-bodied snake has dark brown, black-bordered blotches down it back.
Habitat: Subtropical wetlands and forests.
Comments: First sighted in Everglades National Park in the 1980's, there are now tens of thousands found throughout Florida. Preys on a wide variety of species and is likely responsible for the severe decline in mammal populations in the Everglades.

EASTERN GARTER SNAKE
Thamnophis sirtalis sirtalis
Size: To 4 ft. (1.2 m)
Description: Black, brown, turquoise or greenish snake has three yellowish stripes and a double row of alternating dark spots between the stripes. Coloration is highly variable, but in Florida it is usually blue-green.
Habitat: Near water in meadows, farmlands and valleys.
Comments: A good swimmer, it is often found near water where it feeds on amphibians, small fish and invertebrates.

VENOMOUS SNAKES

FLORIDA COTTONMOUTH
Agkistrodon piscivorus conanti
Size: To 6 ft. (1.8 m)
Description: Large water snake has a spade-shaped head. Edges of mouth are tan. Younger snake has dark blotches on a lighter background. Older individual may be uniformly brown, red-brown or black.
Habitat: Flooded woodlands, lakes, swamps, bayous, rivers, streams.
Comments: Bite is very venomous. When disturbed, it gapes widely and displays the whitish inside of its mouth. Also called water moccasin, it swims with its head out of the water.

Coral Snake

Scarlet Kingsnake

EASTERN CORAL SNAKE
Micrurus fulvius
Size: To 4 ft. (1.2 m)
Description: Unmistakable black, yellow and red banded snake with a black snout. Note how red and yellow bands touch one another.
Habitat: Fields, pastures, hillsides; in or near water.
Comments: An extremely poisonous snake with paralyzing venom. The similar, harmless scarlet kingsnake (*Lampropeltis triangulum elapsoides)* has yellow bands bordered in black. The safety rhyme to remember is "red on yellow can kill a fellow."

DUSKY PYGMY RATTLESNAKE
Sistrurus miliarius barbouri
Size: To 31 in. (78 cm)
Description: Small, slender snake has a grayish body, three rows of side spots and alternating reddish brown and black spots along back.
Habitat: Variable near water.
Comments: The most commonly encountered Florida rattler, it is also the one most often responsible for biting people.

EASTERN DIAMONDBACK RATTLESNAKE
Crotalus adamanteus
Size: To 8 ft. (2.4 m)
Description: Large, heavy-bodied snake has flattened head and dark, diamond-shaped blotches down its back. Tail ends in a rattle.
Habitat: Pine and palmetto flatlands, dry areas, suburbs.
Comments: The largest rattlesnake in the U.S. and the most venomous. A pit viper, it has heat sensing areas between its eyes and nostrils which help it to detect prey. Enlarged front fangs have hollow canals which inject venom into prey when it strikes.

SALAMANDERS

Salamanders are smooth-skinned, tailed amphibians that lack claws and ear openings. Some have the ability to regenerate tails or limbs lost to predators. Seldom seen, they live in dark, moist habitats and are nocturnal and secretive. They are most active in the spring and fall. There are 32 species found in Florida.

SLIMY SALAMANDER
Plethodon grobmani
Size: To 8 in. (20 cm)
Description: Shiny blue-black skin is flecked with light spots.
Habitat: Wet habitats in or under ground litter.

Comments: Frequently observed on cool, wet days. It feeds primarily on worms and small invertebrates. Skin is covered with a sticky substance that is capable of gluing the mouths of its predators shut. Found in northern Florida.

FROGS & TOADS

Frogs and toads are squat, tailless amphibians common near ponds and lakes. All have large heads, large eyes, long hind legs and long, sticky tongues which they use to catch insects. Most have well-developed ears and strong voices. Only males are vocal. There are 30 species found in Florida.

Frogs have smooth skin, slim waists, prominent dorsal ridges and lack parotoid glands. Toads can be distinguished from frogs by their dry, warty skin and prominent glands behind their eyes (parotoids). Some also have swellings between their eyes (bosses). When handled roughly by would-be predators, the warts and glands secrete a poisonous substance which makes the toads extremely unpalatable. Contrary to popular belief, handling toads does not cause warts.

SOUTHERN LEOPARD FROG
Lithobates sphenocephalus
Size: To 5 in. (13 cm)
Description: Green to brown frog has dark-spotted back and two light dorsal ridges. Note small yellow spot in center of tympanum (eardrum).
Habitat: Margins of waterways and ponds, wet fields.
Comments: A common frog noted for its leaping ability. Also called grass frog. Call is a series of short croaks.

SOUTHERN CRICKET FROG
Acris gryllus
Size: To 1 in. (3 cm)
Description: Tiny green to brown frog. Many have a light dorsal stripe that splits into a 'Y' behind the eyes. Note pointed snout.
Habitat: Edges of streams, ponds, swamps and ditches.
Comments: Call is a series of shrill, cricket-like chirps that sounds like two marbles clicking together.

GREEN TREEFROG
Hyla cinerea
Size: To 2.5 in. (6 cm)
Description: Bright green to yellowish frog with a light side stripe of variable length.
Habitat: Variable, near water.
Comments: Common near homes, it often climbs windows and screen doors. Also called rain frog, its call is a cowbell-like – *quenk, quenk, quenk.*

BULLFROG
Lithobates catesbeianus
Size: To 8 in. (20 cm)
Description: Large, green-brown frog with large ear openings and a rounded snout.
Habitat: Ponds and lakes with ample vegetation.
Comments: Primarily nocturnal, it is often seen along shorelines. Call is a deep-pitched – jurrrooom. A voracious predator, it will eat anything it can swallow. Found in the northern half of Florida.

PIG FROG
Lithobates grylio
Size: To 6 in. (15 cm)
Description: Key field marks are prominent eardrum, webbed hind feet and pointy snout. Color ranges from brown to green.
Habitat: Marshes, ponds, lakes with covering of vegetation.
Comments: A highly aquatic frog that rarely leaves the water. Call is a pig-like grunt.

SOUTHERN TOAD
Anaxyrus terrestris
Size: To 4.5 in. (11 cm)
Description: Stout grayish brown to reddish toad has prominent knobs behind its eyes.
Habitat: Found in a variety of habitats with loose soil.
Comments: Common in urban areas, it is often spotted foraging at night near homes and crossing roadways. Sleeps in burrows during the day. Call is a high trill.

OAK TOAD
Anaxyrus quercicus
Size: To 1.25 in. (3.5 cm)
Description: America's smallest toad has a prominent white-to-orange stripe down its back. Note dark blotches on back.
Habitat: Sandy areas.
Comments: Call sounds like a loud chick peeping.

WHAT ARE FISHES?

Fishes are cold-blooded vertebrates that live in water and breathe dissolved oxygen through organs called gills. They are generally characterized by their size, shape, feeding habits, and water temperature preference. Most live in either salt water or fresh water, though a few species divide their lives between the two (these are referred to as anadromous fishes).

All fishes have streamlined bodies covered in scales, and swim by flexing their bodies from side to side. Their fins help to steer while swimming and can also act as brakes. Many species possess an internal air bladder which acts as a depth regulator. By secreting gases into the bladder or absorbing gases from it, they are able to control the depth at which they swim.

Most fish reproduce by laying eggs freely in the water. In many, the male discharges sperm over the eggs as they are laid by the female. Depending on the species, eggs may float, sink, become attached to vegetation, or be buried.

HOW TO IDENTIFY FISHES

First, note the size, shape and color of the fish. Are there any distinguishing field marks like the double dorsal fins of the basses or the downturned lips of the suckers? Is the body thin or torpedo-shaped? Note the orientation and placement of fins on the body. Consult the text to confirm identification.

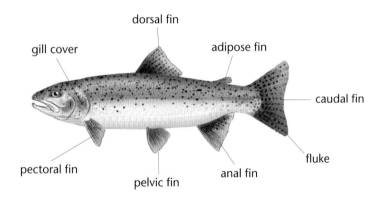

dorsal fin

gill cover

adipose fin

caudal fin

fluke

pectoral fin

pelvic fin

anal fin

LAMPREYS

Lampreys are members of the most primitive order of jawless fishes.

SEA LAMPREY
Petromyzon marinus
Size: To 33 in. (83 cm)
Description: Slender eel-like fish has two long dorsal fins and seven pairs of gill openings. Mouth is sucker-like.
Habitat: Fresh and salt water coastal areas, open ocean.
Comments: Usually seen attached to other fish, it rasps a hole through its host's skin with its tongue and feeds on its body fluids.

SHARKS & ALLIES

These fishes lack bones and have skeletons completely composed of cartilage. They also lack an internal air bladder and must swim continuously or sink to the bottom.

NURSE SHARK
Ginglymostoma cirratum
Size: To 14 ft. (4.2 m)
Description: Gray-brown shark has two dorsal fins and a long barbel attached to each nostril.
Habitat: Inshore waters.
Comments: Common in shallow waters in southern Florida. It uses its barbels to locate prey along the sea floor including crustaceans and small fish. Considered harmless to humans.

GARS

Elongate fish are covered with tough, diamond-shaped scales.

GAR
Lepisosteus spp.
Size: To 10 ft. (3 m)
Description: Slender, dark-spotted fish has a long, toothy snout. Dorsal and anal fins are located far back on body.
Habitat: Sluggish streams and pools with sandy or muddy bottoms.
Comments: Florida is home to four similar-looking species of gar that differ mostly in size.

BOWFINS

The ancestors of this single surviving species swam with dinosaurs.

BOWFIN
Amia calva
Size: To 34 in. (85 cm)
Description: Torpedo-shaped fish has a long dorsal fin extending for more than half its total body length. Note rounded tail.
Habitat: Sluggish streams, swamps, vegetated lakes.
Comments: A transitional species, bowfins possess characteristics of both primitive and modern fishes including a skeleton that is partially composed of cartilage.

BONEFISHES & ALLIES

Members of this group of popular sport fishes have a single dorsal fin and a well-forked tail.

BONEFISH
Albula vulpes
Size: To 3 ft. (90 cm)
Description: Elongate silvery-blue fish with a prominent snout that overhangs the mouth.
Habitat: Shallow coastal waters with muddy or sandy bottoms.
Comments: A solitary fish, it feeds along the bottom for crabs, shrimps and clams. An important game fish.

TARPON
Megalops atlanticus
Size: To 8 ft. (2.4 m)
Description: Large blue-gray fish with silvery sides and a short dorsal fin with a thread-like trailing edge. Scales are unusually large.
Habitat: Shallow coastal waters.
Comments: Considered the king of sportfish by many, it is a powerful swimmer that makes spectacular leaps after being hooked.

EELS

All have snake-like bodies and elongate, spineless fins.

GREEN MORAY
Gymnothorax funebris
Size: To 6 ft. (1.8 m)
Description: Large pea-green
eel has a continuous dorsal
and anal fin.
Habitat: Coral reefs,
harbors, nearshore waters.
Comments: While they appear
threatening, morays are not
aggressive to people unless provoked.
One of several morays found in Florida.

AMERICAN EEL
Anguilla rostrata
Size: To 5 ft. (1.5 m)
Description: Typically dark
green-brown in color, its body
shape is distinctive.
Habitat: Fresh and brackish water.
Comments: It spends its life (up to
15 years) in nearshore and inland
waters before migrating to the sea to
spawn and die. Popular food fish in
Europe and Japan, it is eaten fresh,
pickled and smoked.

HERRINGS & ALLIES

Found in large schools, most are important forage and bait fishes.

ATLANTIC MENHADEN
Brevoortia tyrannus
Size: To 18 in. (45 cm)
Description: Deeply compressed
fish is blue-brown above with
silvery sides. Note large head
and deeply forked tail.
Habitat: Near surface of
inshore and offshore waters.
Comments: Found in huge schools,
it is commercially harvested for its oil.

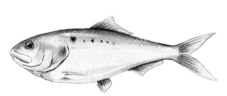

ANCHOVIES

Slender, silvery fishes support commercial fisheries and are an important source of food for sea birds and other fishes.

STRIPED ANCHOVY
Anchoa hepsetus
Size: To 6 in. (15 cm)
Description: Key field marks for this small, silvery fish are its large eyes and pointed snout that overhangs the mouth.
Habitat: Nearshore waters, usually in dense schools.
Comments: Common bait fish that is harvested commercially for its meat and oil.

MINNOWS & ALLIES

Family of primarily small fishes are important forage for game fish and are often sold as bait.

GOLDEN SHINER
Notemigonus crysoleucas
Size: To 12 in. (30 cm)
Description: Deep-bodied, narrow fish with silvery-olive sides and light-colored fins. Belly is keeled between the pelvic and anal fin. Mouth is upturned slightly.
Habitat: Vegetated pools, streams, rivers and ponds.
Comments: Common bait fish often found in schools near the shore.

Common Carp

COMMON CARP
Cyprinus carpio
Size: To 4 ft. (1.2 m)
Description: A large-scaled, deep-bodied olive fish with mouth barbels (whiskers) and a forked, orangish tail.
Habitat: Found in clear and turbid streams, ponds and sloughs. Prefers warm water.
Comments: Introduced species is widely distributed throughout the U.S. Its cousin the grass carp (*Ctenopharyngodon idella*) is commonly used to control algal growth in ponds and lakes.

Grass Carp

PIKES

These predatory fishes are easily distinguished by their duck-like snout. Dorsal and anal fins are located far back on the body.

CHAIN PICKEREL
Esox niger
Size: To 30 in. (75 cm)
Description: Olive-to-brown fish has an elongate snout and sides marked with a dark, chain-like pattern. Undersides are whitish.
Habitat: Streams, rivers and lakes with abundant vegetation in the northern half of Florida.
Comments: Feeds primarily on fish but will eat any animal it can swallow. Jaw is full of sharp, recurved teeth. The similar redfin pickerel (*E. americanus americanus*) has red-orange fins.

Chain Pickerel

Redfin Pickerel

CATFISHES

Most members of this large family of bottomfeeders have scale-less bodies, prominent mouth barbels and sharp spines at the leading edge of the dorsal and pectoral spines.

BROWN BULLHEAD
Ameiurus nebulosus
Size: To 20 in. (50 cm)
Description: Torpedo-shaped mottled brown fish with a rounded anal fin and dark chin barbels.
Habitat: Clear, vegetated streams, pools, backwaters.
Comments: Unlike many catfish, it is relatively intolerant of turbid or polluted waters. Native to Florida, it has been widely introduced throughout the U.S.

CHANNEL CATFISH
Ictalurus punctatus
Size: To 4 ft. (1.2 m)
Description: Olive to blue-gray catfish has dark spots scattered on its back and sides.
Habitat: Deep pools in rivers.
Comments: A popular food and game fish, it is the species most commonly raised in hatcheries. Widely introduced throughout the U.S.

LIVEBEARERS

Unlike most fishes, livebearers are fertilized internally and give birth to live young.

MOSQUITOFISH
Gambusia affinis
Size: To 2.5 in. (6 cm)
Description: Gray to brownish fish with bluish sides. Has dusky teardrop near eye and 1-3 rows of dark spots on dorsal fin and tail.
Habitat: Ponds, lakes, slow-moving streams.
Comments: Feeds on mosquito larvae and has been widely introduced to control mosquito populations.

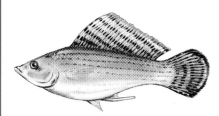

SAILFIN MOLLY
Poecilia latipinna
Size: To 5 in. (13 cm)
Description: The male is distinguished at a glance by its huge, spotted, orange-edged dorsal fin and spotted sides.
Habitat: Fresh and brackish marshes, ponds, sloughs and pools.
Comments: Very common in peninsular Florida, it is able to tolerate changes in water temperature and salinity. A popular aquarium fish.

SILVERSIDES

Small fishes have a silvery side stripe and two dorsal fins.

BROOK SILVERSIDES
Labidesthes sicculus
Size: To 4 in. (10 cm)
Description: Silvery fish has a flattened head and a beak-like mouth. Note side stripe and two dorsal fins.
Habitat: Clear streams, creeks and lakes, usually near the surface.
Comments: Abundant and widespread throughout Florida, it travels in large schools. An important forage and bait fish.

SQUIRRELFISHES

Eleven members of this family of predominantly red reef fishes are found in Florida waters.

LONGSPINE SQUIRRELFISH
Holocentrus rufus
Size: To 12 in. (30 cm)
Description: Bright red or red-striped reef fish. First dorsal fin is spiny and almost separate from the soft second dorsal fin.
Habitat: Shallow coral reefs.
Comments: Most active at night when feeding, it can be easily seen hiding in coral reefs during the day.

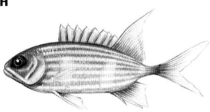

PIPEFISH

Family of slender fishes all have skeletons composed of bony rings.

GULF PIPEFISH
Syngnathus scovelli
Size: To 7 in. (18 cm)
Description: Very slim, snake-like fish.
Habitat: Grassy beds in salt and fresh water.
Comments: Related to seahorses, pipefish are most often seen near shore.

PERCH ORDER

This general category includes members of the largest order of bony fishes, perciformes. All have dorsal and anal fins that possess spines. Because of this, they are often referred to as spiny-rayed fishes.

LARGEMOUTH BASS
Micropterus salmoides
Size: To 38 in. (95 cm)
Description: Greenish, mottled fish with a dark, often blotched, side stripe. Has a large mouth with the upper jaw extending past the eye.
Habitat: Quiet, vegetated lakes, ponds and rivers.
Comments: The most popular freshwater sport fish in Florida, it weighs up to 22 lbs. (10 kg). The similar smallmouth bass (*M. dolomieu*) has blotched sides and its jaw does not extend beyond the eye.

Largemouth

Florida's State Freshwater Fish

Smallmouth

SNOOK
Centropomus undecimalis
Size: To 4.5 ft. (1.4 m)
Description: Elongate, slender fish is green-brown above and whitish below. Key field marks are its pointed snout, jutting lower jaw and dark side stripe.
Habitat: Fresh and salt water coastal areas, rivers.
Comments: A sleek and fast fish, it is popular with anglers. Feeds primarily on crustaceans and fish.

STRIPED BASS
Morone saxatilis
Size: To 6 ft. (1.8 m)
Description: Grayish fish has 6-8 dark side stripes. First dorsal fin has 8-10 stiff spines.
Habitat: Nearshore coastal waters.
Comments: Lives in salt water, spawns in fresh water. A popular sport fish, its numbers have declined significantly in recent years due to overfishing.

RED GROUPER
Epinephelus morio
Size: To 3 ft. (90 cm)
Description: Robust red-brown fish with pale blotches on its body and dark spots around its eyes.
Habitat: Coral reefs to depths of 500 ft. (150 m).
Comments: A very popular sport and food fish that is harvested commercially. One of 20 similar species of grouper found in Florida's coastal waters.

SWAMP DARTER
Etheostoma fusiforme
Size: To 2 in. (5 cm)
Description: Small, elongate, olive-brown fish has 10-12 dark squarish blotches on its sides. Caudal fin has 3 dark spots at its base.
Habitat: Clear or muddy waters, ponds, marshes.
Comments: One of the most common of several species of darters found in Florida.

REDBREAST SUNFISH
Lepomis auritus
Size: To 11 in. (28 cm)
Description: It is olive green above with pale yellowish sides. Key field marks are reddish belly and black ear flap.
Habitat: Quiet, clear lakes, ponds and rivers in northern Florida.
Comments: Another common sunfish is the redear sunfish (*L. microlophus*). It is distinguished by a red mark near its earflap. The redear feeds on snails that it crushes with molar-like teeth and is also known as shellcracker.

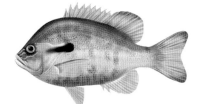

Redbreast Sunfish

Redear Sunfish

BLACK CRAPPIE
Pomoxis nigromaculatus
Size: To 20 in. (50 cm)
Description: Greenish, mottled fish with dorsal fin set well back on its hunched back. First of two dorsal fins has 7-8 stiff spines.
Habitat: Quiet, clear lakes, ponds and rivers.
Comments: Also tolerant of silty water, it is caught in a wide range of habitats. The similar white crappie (*P. annularis*), also common in Florida, has 6 spines in its first dorsal fin.

Black Crappie

White Crappie

BLUEGILL
Lepomis macrochirus
Size: To 16 in. (40 cm)
Description: Flattened brassy fish with long pectoral fins and a dark-spotted dorsal fin. Dusky side bars are often present.
Habitat: Quiet, vegetated lakes and ponds, rivers.
Comments: One of the most popular sport fishes in the country, it is often stocked in lakes and impoundments.

SPOTFIN BUTTERFLYFISH
Chaetodon ocellatus
Size: To 8 in. (20 cm)
Description: Flattened, deep-bodied whitish fish with yellowish fins and a prominent spot at the base of its second dorsal fin.
Habitat: Coral and rocky reefs in shallow water.
Comments: Usually swims in the vicinity of structures that offer cover if needed. Feeds on coral polyps and sea anemones.

BLUEHEAD
Thalassoma bifasciatum
Size: To 6 in. (15 cm)
Description: The male of this aptly named fish has a blue head bordered by black rings and a green body. A yellowish phase also occurs that has two large reddish spots behind each eye.
Habitat: Coral reefs, nearshore waters, bays.
Comments: The bluehead is one of many small, colorful fish that are common near coral reefs.

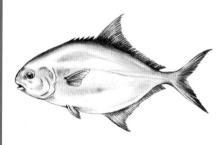

FLORIDA POMPANO
Trachinotus carolinus
Size: To 25 in. (63 cm)
Description: Deep-bodied fish is blue-green above with silvery sides. Belly is often yellowish. Blunt snout overhangs small mouth.
Habitat: Shallow nearshore waters.
Comments: Popular food and sport fish is a fast swimmer known for its leaping ability. Often caught by surf-casters. Also called cobbler.

ATLANTIC SPADEFISH
Chaetodipterus faber
Size: To 3 ft. (90 cm)
Description: Deep-bodied fish is distinguished by its striped sides and long dorsal and anal fins.
Habitat: Coral reefs, nearshore waters.
Comments: Usually swims in large schools.

SHEEPSHEAD
Archosargus probatocephalus
Size: To 3 ft. (90 cm)
Description: Small-mouthed fish has 5-6 prominent vertical dark bars across gray-yellow body.
Habitat: Shallow, nearshore waters, often near piers.
Comments: Named for its protruding, sheep-like incisor teeth used to break open crustaceans and shellfish. A popular food fish.

SCHOOLMASTER
Lutjanus apodus
Size: To 2 ft. (60 cm)
Description: Gray-brown above, light below with a number of broad vertical bars on its sides. All fins are yellowish.
Habitat: Shallow, nearshore waters.
Comments: Also called black snapper and sea lawyer, it is common near coral reefs. Feeds on crabs, shrimp, mollusks and fish.

PINFISH
Lagodon rhomboides
Size: To 16 in. (40 cm)
Description: Bluish-brassy fish has a number of pale yellowish side stripes and a dark shoulder spot.
Habitat: Shallow, nearshore waters, often near piers.
Comments: Very common in coastal areas where shellfish are abundant.

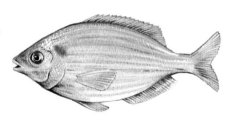

BLACK DRUM
Pogonias cromis
Size: To 6 ft. (1.8 m)
Description: Deep-bodied gray-to-bronze fish with black fins and 4-5 broad, dark side bars. Note long chin barbels.
Habitat: Surf zones, open ocean.
Comments: Has prominent teeth which it uses to crush the shells of mollusks and crustaceans. Often caught in nearshore waters by surf-casters and bridge anglers.

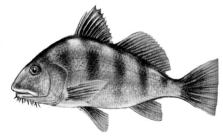

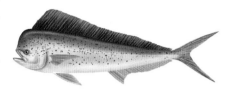

DOLPHINFISH
Coryphaena hippurus
Size: To 7 ft. (2.1 m)
Description: Distinguished at a glance by its high forehead and long dorsal and anal fins.
Habitat: Deep water offshore.
Comments: Also called dolphin and dorado.

GAFFTOPSAIL CATFISH
Bagre marinus
Size: To 40 in. (1 m)
Description: Bluish-silvery, scaleless fish has long filaments extending from the dorsal and pectoral fins. Note adipose fin and prominent chin barbels.
Habitat: Nearshore waters, estuaries.
Comments: Spines on dorsal and pectoral fins can inflict painful injuries. Most rarely exceed 2 ft. (60 cm) in length.

SERGEANT MAJOR
Abudefduf saxatilis
Size: To 7 in. (18 cm)
Description: Small, blue-silvery fish is yellowish above and has 5 dark side stripes.
Habitat: Shallow nearshore waters, often near docks and piers.
Comments: An abundant nearshore fish, it feeds on algae, barnacles and other invertebrates.

STRIPED MULLET
Mugil cephalus
Size: To 18 in. (45 cm)
Description: Torpedo-shaped, olive-to-bluish fish with two, small, widely spaced dorsal fins.
Habitat: Nearshore waters, open ocean.
Comments: Migrates in enormous schools and is an important commercial species. Found primarily in coastal waters, some venture inland along rivers. An oily fish, it is also called fatback.

GREAT BARRACUDA
Sphyraena barracuda
Size: To 6 ft. (1.8 m)
Description: Torpedo-shaped blue-gray fish has a long snout, jutting lower jaw and prominent teeth. Sides are covered with dark blotches.
Habitat: Offshore waters to depths of 60 ft. (18 m).
Comments: This mean-looking fish is relatively harmless but should be treated with caution. A prized sport fish, it is also called sea tiger and sea pike.

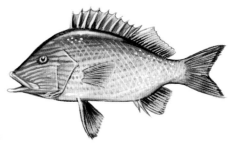

WHITE GRUNT
Haemulon plumierii
Size: To 18 in. (45 cm)
Description: Bronze fish is distinguished by the wavy blue lines along its body.
Habitat: Coral reefs, grassy and sandy bottomed bays.
Comments: Exhibits a 'kissing' behavior when two fish face each other with their mouths open and make lip contact.

LOOKDOWN
Selene vomer
Size: To 16 in. (40 cm)
Description: Flattened metallic fish has a very steep head profile and long dorsal and anal fin spines.
Habitat: Shallow coastal waters with sandy or muddy bottoms.
Comments: School-forming fish is an aquarium favorite found throughout the Caribbean and Gulf coast waters.

COBIA
Rachycentron canadum
Size: To 7 ft. (2.1 m)
Description: Silvery fish has black fins and a jutting lower jaw. The first dorsal fin is a series of 7-9 short spines. Second dorsal fin and anal fin are long and curved.
Habitat: Offshore waters, coral reefs.
Comments: A popular game fish that will take almost any bait.

QUEEN ANGELFISH
Holacanthus ciliaris
Size: To 12 in. (30 cm)
Description: Disc shaped, orange-blue fish with a yellowish tail. Note large, black, blue-ringed forehead spot.
Habitat: Coral and rocky reefs in shallow water.
Comments: Also called yellow angel, this conspicuous fish is active during the day and is often observed in nearshore waters.

QUEEN PARROTFISH
Scarus vetula
Size: To 20 in. (50 cm)
Description: Colorful greenish fish has yellow-orange highlights. Note bicolored dorsal and anal fins.
Habitat: Coral and rocky reefs in shallow water.
Comments: Named for its fused front teeth that form a beak-like structure that allows them to nip off bits of coral reefs.

BLUE TANG
Acanthurus coeruleus
Size: To 14 in. (35 cm)
Description: Bright blue, oval-shaped fish has a concave tail fin. Named for the sharp, knife-like spine found on each side of the tail base. Young fish are yellow.
Habitat: Coral and rocky reefs in shallow water.
Comments: Also called surgeonfish, it should be handled carefully if hooked.

QUEEN TRIGGERFISH
Balistes vetula
Size: To 20 in. (50 cm)
Description: Striking gray-blue fish has a yellow belly, two bright blue stripes on its snout and a series of smaller stripes radiating away from its eye.
Habitat: Coral and rocky reefs in shallow water, vegetated areas.
Comments: Its sharp dorsal spines protect the fish by making it difficult to capture and swallow.

BLUE MARLIN
Makaira nigricans
Size: To 14 ft. (4.2 m)
Description: Torpedo-shaped fish, blue above and light below, is distinguished by its sickle-shaped dorsal fin and steep head profile.
Habitat: Open ocean.
Comments: A fast swimmer, it feeds on tuna, squid and bonito. The similar striped marlin (*Tetrapturus audax*) has dark side bars. Most marlin landed weigh under 200 lbs. (90 kg) but may reach 1,500 lb. (680 kg).

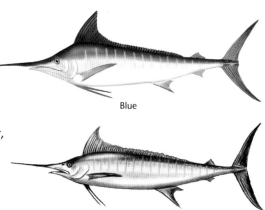

Blue

Striped

SAILFISH
Istiophorous platypterus
Size: To 10 ft. (3 m)
Description: Blue above and white below, it is distinguished at a glance by its huge blue dorsal fin and elongate snout.
Habitat: Open ocean.
Comments: A prized sport fish that is renowned for its fighting ability.

Florida's State Saltwater Fish

FLATFISHES

Flat fish with both eyes on the same side of the body. They typically lie on the bottom buried in sediment with just their eyes exposed.

GULF FLOUNDER
Paralichthys albigutta
Size: To 17 in. (43 cm)
Description: Distinguished by its flat profile and long dorsal and anal fins. Note the 3 dark spots that form a triangle on its back.
Habitat: Estuaries, mud flats, off-shore waters, occasionally rivers.
Comments: Related to numerous similar species of flatfishes found off the Florida coast. An important food and game fish.

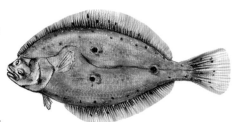

WHAT IS SEASHORE LIFE?

This section includes a variety of animal and plant groups that can be found along the Atlantic and Gulf coasts of Florida. Most species can be readily observed in tidal pools or shallow waters. All of the animals in this section are classed as invertebrates, or animals without backbones.

The best time to observe the greatest variety of species is during low tide. Tide times are often published in newspapers, and tide tables are available at most marinas and sporting goods stores. There are generally two tides a day, and tidal differences vary from about 8 ft. (2.4 m) on the north Atlantic side to 3 ft. (.9 m) at Florida's big bend on the Gulf coast. The lowest tides of the year occur in midwinter and midsummer.

The main groups covered in this section include marine plants, coelenterates, sea stars and allies, crustaceans and mollusks.

High Tide

eelgrass
barnacles
shore crabs

Mid Tide

sea urchins
sea stars
clams
oysters
snails
sand dollars

Low Tide

turtle grass
crabs
sea stars
sea urchins
sand dollars
scallops

Subtidal Zone

SEASHORE PLANTS

This general group includes a few of the most common coastal marine and dune plants.

TURTLE GRASS
Thalassia testudinum
Size: To 12 in. (30 cm)
Description: Broad, grass-like leaves grow in clusters and often form large underwater 'meadows'.
Habitat: Shallow water along southern and Gulf coasts.
Comments: An important species that provides food and cover to a wide variety of marine organisms.

SARGASSUM WEED
Sargassum **spp.**
Size: To 33 ft. (10 m)
Description: Marine plant has numerous small air bladders attached to the stems to keep the plant afloat.
Habitat: Deep offshore waters.
Comments: Sargassum weed grows in huge forests in offshore waters. Fronds continually detach and are washed ashore by Gulf currents.

EELGRASS
Zostera marina
Size: To 5 ft. (1.5 m)
Description: Tall slender plant with grass-like leaves.
Habitat: Shallow bays and estuaries on muddy and sandy bottoms.
Comments: A favorite food of ducks and geese, its leaves are often encrusted with small marine animals and insects.

GLASSWORT
Salicornia **spp.**
Size: To 12 in. (30 cm)
Description: Mat-forming plant comprised of translucent green branching stems. The stem tips turn bright red or yellow in autumn.
Habitat: Salt marshes.
Comments: An extremely hardy plant that is able to grow where other marsh plants cannot survive.

SEA OATS
Uniola paniculata
Size: To 6 ft. (1.8 m)
Description: Tall grass has a large spreading flower and seed head.
Habitat: Sand dunes.
Comments: A pioneer plant, its spreading roots help to anchor dunes in place.

SALT MARSH CORDGRASS
Spartina alterniflora
Size: To 8 ft. (2.4 m)
Description: Tall grass is one of the dominant plants in coastal bays and estuaries. Leaves are linear and flat.
Habitat: Brackish nearshore waters.
Comments: Cordgrass communities support many animals that live exclusively in that environment.

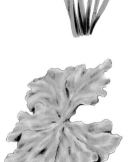

SEA LETTUCE
Ulva lactuca
Size: To 2 ft. (60 cm)
Description: Bright green, lettuce-like algae blade.
Habitat: Intertidal zone.
Comments: An edible algae high in vitamins, it is eaten for food around the world.

COELENTERATES

This group contains a variety of free-swimming and colonial creatures including jellyfish, hydroids, anemones and corals.

PORTUGESE MAN-OF-WAR
Physalia physalis
Size: To 5 in. (13 cm) wide
Description: Distinguished by its blue-purple float and numerous, multi-colored stinging tentacles up to 50 ft. (15 m) long.
Habitat: Surface of the ocean along eastern and southern Florida.
Comments: Tentacles contain highly toxic poison that can inflict burns requiring hospitalization. Tentacles can harm even after the animal is dead.

MOON JELLYFISH
Aurelia aurita
Size: To 16 in. (40 cm) wide
Description: Globular, translucent bell-shaped body with a fringe of numerous, stinging tentacles.
Habitat: Surface of the ocean.
Comments: Commonly washes ashore following storms. Stinging tentacles can cause an itchy rash.

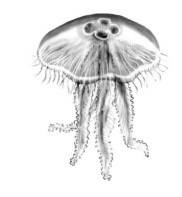

SAIL JELLYFISH
Velella velella
Size: To 3 in. (8 cm) wide
Description: Small jellyfish has a translucent triangular crest on its upper surface that acts like a sail.
Habitat: Surface of the ocean.
Comments: Also called by-the-wind-sailor, it frequently washes ashore. Sting is relatively harmless to people.

LABYRINTHINE BRAIN CORAL
Diploria labyrinthiformis
Size: To 8 ft. (2.4 m) tall
Description: Distinctive stony coral has a wrinkled surface that resembles a human brain.
Habitat: Coral reefs in shallow water.
Comments: A living colony of anemone-like polyps live in protective cups on the surface of the coral. To feed, they extend feathery tentacles out of the cups to capture floating plankton.

STAGHORN CORAL
Acropora cervicornis
Size: To 10 ft. (3 m)
Description: Branching, tree-like coral is yellowish to brown-purple with light-colored stem tips.
Habitat: Protected areas along reefs.
Comments: Often sold as a souvenir, it has been severely depleted in some southern areas. Florida has about a dozen corals that provide important sources of cover for fishes and invertebrates.

SEA STARS & ALLIES

These mostly bottom-dwelling animals are characterized by spiny bodies and radial symmetry, i.e., body parts repeat around a central hub. The 'arms' are usually arranged in multiples of 5, and may be short or long, cylindrical or flattened. Size refers to width.

COMMON SEA STAR
Asterias forbesi
Size: To 12 in. (30 cm)
Description: Long-armed, brown to olive-colored sea star is covered with short spines.
Habitat: Variable, ranging from tidepools to deep waters.
Comments: Feeds mostly on clams, oysters and other bivalve mollusks. It uses the suction-like disks on its arms to pull the shells open and then extends its stomach out of its mouth and digests prey in its shell.

CUSHION STAR
Oreaster reticulatus
Size: To 18 in. (45 cm)
Description: Deep-bodied sea star has five short, broad 'arms'. Adults are brownish or reddish and have a network of light-colored lines on their body. Young are greenish.
Habitat: Sandy bottoms in shallow water.
Comments: The largest and best-known Atlantic sea star. Over-collecting has seriously depleted its numbers in some areas in recent years.

KEYHOLE URCHIN (SAND DOLLAR)
Mellita quinquiesperforata
Size: To 5 in. (13 cm)
Description: Flattened brown body is covered with short spines. Has 2 pairs of smaller slots and a single larger one.
Habitat: Found at low tides on sandy beaches, often partially buried.
Comments: Sand dollar skeletons are often found washed ashore. Note flower-like impression on shell.

Skeleton

LONG-SPINED SEA URCHIN
Diadema antillarum
Size: Body to 4 in. (10 cm)
Description: Distinguished by oval body and long purplish-to-black spines up to 16 in. (40 cm) long.
Habitat: Coral reefs.
Comments: Spines are very sharp and easily puncture fingers, swim fins and wetsuits, causing painful stings.

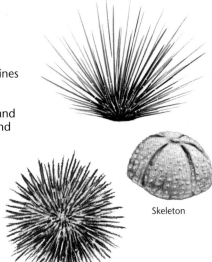

ATLANTIC PURPLE SEA URCHIN
Arbacia punctulata
Size: Body to 2 in. (5 cm)
Description: Purplish urchin is distinguished by its short spines 1 in. (3 cm) long.
Habitat: Intertidal waters.
Comments: The skeletons of urchins are often found washed ashore.

Skeleton

CRUSTACEANS

Most crustaceans live in or near saltwater and have a hard external skeleton, antennae and paired limbs. The limbs differ greatly in form and function, and are modified for specific purposes in different species.

BLUE CRAB
Callinectes sapidus
Size: To 9 in. (23 cm)
Description: Delicately-hued bluish-gray crab. Males have blue 'fingers' at end of claws; females have red 'fingers'.
Habitat: Intertidal waters.
Comments: A popular seafood crab, it supports the state's third largest commercial fishery.

FIDDLER CRAB
Uca spp.
Size: To 1.5 in. (4 cm)
Description: A small, square-bodied crab. Males are easily distinguished by their single huge pincer.
Habitat: Intertidal waters, beaches.
Comments: Several similar species of fiddler crab are found in Florida. The large pincer is primarily used for its courtship displays.

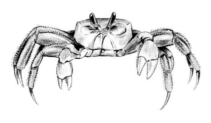

GHOST CRAB
Ocypode quadrata
Size: To 2 in. (5 cm)
Description: Square-bodied crab is yellowish- to tan-colored and blends with the sand.
Habitat: Sandy beaches.
Comments: These crabs are often seen scuttling swiftly along beaches and are especially active on moonlit nights.

HORSESHOE CRAB
Limulus polyphemus
Size: To 12 in. (30 cm) wide
Description: Unmistakable horseshoe-shaped crab has a pointed tail up to 2 ft. (60 cm) long.
Habitat: Intertidal waters on muddy and sandy bottoms to depths of 70 ft. (21 m).
Comments: Large numbers often congregate in nearshore waters during spring mating season. Not a true crab, it is more closely related to spiders.

HERMIT CRAB
Pagurus spp.
Size: To 2 in. (5 cm)
Description: Small crab lives in a discarded snail shell. It has two pair of walking legs and a pair of pincers.
Habitat: Common intertidally in tide pools or on mud or sand.
Comments: Several similar-looking species of hermit crabs are found along Atlantic and Gulf shores.

BEACH FLEA
Talorchestia spp.
Size: To 1 in. (3 cm)
Description: Small sand-colored, jumping, bug-like crustacean.
Habitat: Near the high tide line and above, often in seaweed or under debris.
Comments: Once disturbed, these hoppers scatter by leaping distances of up to 12 in. (30 cm).

GREAT LAND CRAB
Cardisoma guanhumi
Size: To 5 in. (13 cm)
Description: Green-to-orange crab has a smooth, globe-shaped body. Males have claws of vastly different sizes.
Habitat: Muddy areas, mangroves.
Comments: This edible species is a popular table item throughout the Caribbean.

PINK SHRIMP
Penaeus duorarum
Size: To 8 in. (20 cm)
Description: Slender gray to red-brown crustacean has five pairs of jointed legs and long antennae. Tail has two lobes.
Habitat: Intertidal waters to depths of 300 ft. (91 m).
Comments: One of the most important commercial shrimp species in Atlantic and Gulf waters, it is primarily nocturnal and must be harvested at night.

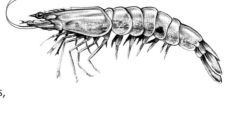

ACORN BARNACLE
Balanus spp.
Size: To 3 in. (8 cm)
Description: Volcano-like gray shell often grows in clusters attached to piers and structures at the high tide line.
Habitat: Coastal.
Comments: It feeds by opening plates at the top of its shell and extending feathery legs to trap small organisms.

GOOSENECK BARNACLE
Lepas anatifera
Size: To 6 in. (15 cm)
Description: Flexible, fleshy stalk topped with flattened body composed of joined, hard, whitish plates.
Habitat: Attached to floating objects.
Comments: Often found attached to debris washed up on beaches.

MOLLUSKS

This large group of soft-bodied and usually hard-shelled invertebrates occupies many habitats in water and on land. The mouth of most mollusks – excluding bivalves – has a ribbon-like toothed structure called a radula which helps the animals break down food or capture prey.

FLORIDA LACE MUREX
Chicoreus florifer dilectus
Size: To 3 in. (8 cm)
Description: Whitish-to-tan shell has raised lacy margins.
Habitat: Shallow water, intertidal areas.
Comments: Florida's most common murex is often found washed up on beaches. A carnivore, it feeds mostly on bivalve mollusks.

FLORIDA HORSE CONCH
Pleuroploca gigantea
Size: To 2 ft. (60 cm)
Description: Large, orange-brown to pinkish, spindle-shaped shell has fine spiral threads.
Habitat: Low tide to 20 ft. (6 m) depths.
Comments: Feeds on other large snail-like creatures by holding its operculum (a kind of trap-door) open, and inserting a tube-like snout that eats the soft parts of the prey.

Florida's State Shell

LIGHTNING WHELK
Busycon contrarium
Size: To 15 in. (38 cm)
Description: Yellowish to grayish shell is streaked with brown and light-colored bands. The only Florida shell that spirals regularly to the left and has the shell opening on the left.
Habitat: On sandy soils from low-tide line to depths of 10 ft. (3 m).
Comments: Feeds on other mollusks by rasping a hole in their shells and feeding on the soft animal inside.

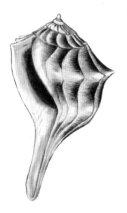

QUEEN HELMET
Cassis madagascariensis
Size: To 16 in. (40 cm)
Description: Yellowish-brown, conch-like shell has rows of prominent knobs on its upper side. The edges of the shell opening are brownish; one side is lined with a series of small ridges.
Habitat: Shallow water with sandy bottoms.
Comments: Cameos are often carved from its heavy shell.

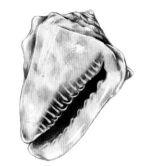

SCOTCH BONNET
Phalium granulatum
Size: To 4 in. (10 cm)
Description: Small yellowish-white conical shell has whorls of square, brown-yellow spots. The inner lips of the shell are thickened and toothed and the insides are white.
Habitat: Shallow water on sand bottoms.
Comments: Most often seen when storms wash large numbers of the shells ashore.

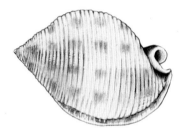

THICK-LIPPED OYSTER DRILL
Eupleura caudata
Size: To 1.5 in. (4 cm)
Description: Small, somewhat flattened shell with prominent ribs. May be white, brown or pinkish.
Habitat: Common near oyster beds.
Comments: Feeds primarily on oysters and often causes severe damage to commercial oyster beds.

WENTLETRAP
Epitonium spp.
Size: To 1.5 in. (4 cm)
Description: Delicate, spiral shell is distinguished by its raised 'ribs'.
Habitat: Nearshore and deep ocean.
Comments: Also called staircase shell, it is most common on beaches in southwestern Florida.

COMMON PURPLE SEA SNAIL
Janthina janthina
Size: To 1.5 in. (4 cm)
Description: Small snail has shell that is whitish-purple above and dark purple below.
Habitat: Floats upside down on the water's surface on a raft of bubbles.
Comments: Usually found in open ocean water, great numbers are often cast up on beaches during storms.

EASTERN OYSTER
Crassostrea virginica
Size: To 10 in. (25 cm)
Description: Distinguished at a glance by its heavy, irregular shell.
Habitat: Intertidal waters.
Comments: A bivalve like clams, mussels and scallops, its body is composed of two hinged shells held together by powerful muscles.

GIANT ATLANTIC COCKLE
Dinocardium robustum
Size: To 5 in. (13 cm)
Description: Deeply ribbed shell is fan-shaped and often has concentric rings of dark spots. Inside of shell is pink.
Habitat: Intertidal to deep water.
Comments: Cockles are also known as heart shells because two shells joined together have a heart-shape when viewed from the side. Several species of cockle are found in Florida.

HOOKED MUSSEL
Ischadium recurvum
Size: To 2 in. (5 cm)
Description: Brown to bluish shell has a series of fine ribs. Tip of shell is strongly hooked.
Habitat: Intertidal waters, often attached to piers and pilings. More common in northern Florida.
Comments: Mussels often grow in association with barnacles. Those located at the tops of pilings indicate the high tide mark.

LETTERED OLIVE
Oliva sayana
Size: To 3 in. (8 cm)
Description: Polished, elongate brownish shell is marked with an intricate pattern of lines and markings that some think resembles lettering.
Habitat: Intertidal to 20 ft. (6 m) depths.
Comments: A pale yellowish phase of this species is prized by collectors.

COMMON EASTERN DOG WHELK
Nassarius vibex
Size: To 1.5 in. (4 cm)
Description: Ribs of spiral shell are beaded. Color ranges from gray to brownish.
Habitat: Shallow water on mud or sand bottoms.
Comments: Also called mud snails, these scavengers are often seen feeding on dead fish washed up on the beach. Also called the mottled dog whelk.

COMMON BABY'S EAR
Sinum perspectivum
Size: To 2 in. (5 cm)
Description: White, snail-like shell has a small spiral. The shell opening is large and ear-shaped.
Habitat: Common in intertidal waters.
Comments: One of a number of popular, collectable moon snails.

SUNRAY VENUS CLAM
Macrocallista nimbosa
Size: To 5 in. (13 cm)
Description: Elongate lavender to tan shell has dark radial markings.
Habitat: Shallow water on sand bottoms.
Comments: Very common. Sun-baked specimens may be pinkish.

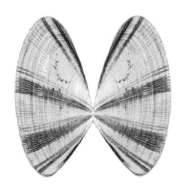

FLORIDA COQUINA
Donax variabilis
Size: To .8 in. (2 cm)
Description: Small, extremely variable shell may have dark markings. Color ranges from white and orange to blue and pink.
Habitat: Common on sandy shores below the surf line.
Comments: Also called butterfly shells, dead shells are often found joined and spread like wings. One of Florida's most common mollusks.

ATLANTIC SLIPPER SNAIL
Crepidula fornicata
Size: To 2 in. (5 cm)
Description: White to tan oval shell has a raised shelf-like structure that makes it resemble a slipper.
Habitat: In shallow water attached to rocks, crabs and other hard objects.
Comments: Living individuals may be stacked on top of each other. Also called boat shell.

ALTERNATE TELLIN
Tellina alternata
Size: To 3 in. (8 cm)
Description: Fattened oval shell is rounded at the front and sharply sloped at the rear. Color may be pink, white or yellow.
Habitat: Sandy bottoms from nearshore to 400 ft. (122 m) deep.
Comments: This is one of the largest of several species of tellin that are commonly washed up on beaches.

SAW-TOOTHED PEN SHELL
Atrina serrata
Size: To 10 in. (25 cm)
Description: Large brownish to yellowish shell is wedge- or fan-shaped.
Habitat: Muddy and sandy bottoms to 20 ft. (6 m) deep.
Comments: Huge shell is easy to spot in beach drift. Shells are brittle and break easily.

ANGEL WING
Cyrtopleura costata
Size: To 8 in. (20 cm)
Description: Large whitish shell may be tinged in pink. Prominent ribs show through as grooves on white underside.
Habitat: Sandy and muddy bottoms to 60 ft. (18 m) deep.
Comments: Very common on the west coast of Florida where it is avidly collected.

COMMON JINGLE SHELL
Anomia simplex
Size: To 2.5 in. (6 cm)
Description: Silvery to yellowish shell has fine concentric growth lines (wrinkles). Interior is pearly.
Habitat: In shallow water attached to piers, rocks and boats.
Comments: Shell is similar in texture and thickness to a toenail.

ATLANTIC BAY SCALLOP
Argopecten irradians
Size: To 3 in. (8 cm)
Description: White to brownish shell is almost circular along the outer edge. Shell has 12-17 radial ribs.
Habitat: Muddy and sandy bottoms to 60 ft. (18 m) deep.
Comments: An important commercial species, its numbers have dwindled in recent years due to habitat loss.

CALICO SCALLOP
Argopecten gibbus
Size: To 2 in. (5 cm)
Description: Fan-shaped shell has deep, squarish ribs. Whitish in color, it has several irregular brown and purple patches.
Habitat: Shallow to deep waters.
Comments: The most common species found along beaches.

WHAT ARE TREES & SHRUBS?

TREES

Trees can be broadly defined as perennial woody plants at least 16 ft. (5 m) tall with a single stem and a well-developed crown of branches, twigs and leaves. Most are long-lived plants and range in age from 40-50 years for smaller deciduous trees to several hundred years for many of the conifers.

A tree's size and shape is largely determined by its genetic makeup, but growth is also affected by environmental factors such as moisture, light and competition from other species. Trees growing in crowded stands will often only support compact crowns due to the competition for light. Some species at high altitudes grow gnarled and twisted as a result of exposure to high winds.

Common Tree Silhouettes

| Pine | Oak | Palm | Maple | Red Mangrove |

SHRUBS

Shrubs are perennial woody plants normally less than 16 ft. (5 m) tall that support a crown of branches, twigs and leaves. Unlike trees, they are anchored to the ground by several stems rather than a single trunk. Most are fast-growing and provide an important source of food and shelter for wildlife.

N.B. – *Some shrubs that are most conspicuous when in bloom are included in the following section on flowering plants.*

HOW TO IDENTIFY TREES AND SHRUBS

First, note its size and shape. Does it have one or several 'trunks?' Examine the size, color, and shape of the leaves and how they are arranged on the twigs. Are they opposite or alternate? Simple or compound? Hairy or smooth? Are flowers or fruits visible on branches or on the ground? Once you've collected as much information as you can, consult the illustrations and text to confirm your sighting.

SIMPLE LEAF SHAPES

Elliptical Heart-shaped Rounded Oval Lobed Lance-shaped

COMPOUND LEAVES

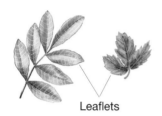

Leaflets

LEAF ARRANGEMENTS

Alternate Opposite Whorled

COMMON FRUITS

Drupe
junipers, cherries,
dogwoods, hollies

Pome
apples, plums,
yuccas, pears

Nut
walnuts,
pecans,
hickories

Berry
blackberries,
raspberries

Winged Seed
dandelions,
milkweeds,
poplars,
cottonwoods

Samara
maples, ashes,
hophornbeams,
elms

Acorn
oaks

Pod
peas,
mesquites,
locusts

PINES

Most have long, needle-like leaves which grow grouped in bundles of 2-5. Male and female cones usually occur on the same tree.

SLASH PINE
Pinus elliottii
Size: To 115 ft. (35 m)
Description: Stout, stiff needles are up to 11 in. (28 cm) long and grouped in bundles of 2-3. Oval cones have scales that terminate in sharp prickles.
Habitat: Flatlands, low hills, bordering waterways.
Comments: An important commercial species, its wood is hard and durable. It grows rapidly and is frequently used in reforestation projects.

LONGLEAF PINE
Pinus palustris
Size: To 130 ft. (40 m)
Description: Straight-trunked tree has very long needles (to 18 in./45 cm) arranged into tight bundles of 3. The needles grow in rounded clusters at the ends of branches, giving the tree a tufted appearance. Cylindrical cones are up to 10 in. (25 cm) long and have thin prickles at the scale tips.
Habitat: Poor soils on prairies and scrub lands.
Comments: A valuable source of food and cover for wildlife.

SAND PINE
Pinus clausa
Size: To 70 ft. (21 m)
Description: Small, often shrubby, pine has a rounded crown. Thin, short needles grow in 2's along twigs. Egg-shaped cones have sharp prickles on their outer edges.
Habitat: Dry sandy soils.
Comments: Found only in Florida, it is common in scrub habitats. It is one of the first species to recolonize burned areas following a forest fire.

CEDARS

All have scaly or awl-shaped leaves that are tightly bunched on twigs. The heavily weighted branchlets often droop at their tips.

SOUTHERN RED CEDAR
Juniperus virginiana silicicola
Size: To 60 ft. (18 m)
Description: 4-sided twigs are covered with overlapping, blue-green scale-like leaves. Fruit is a blue berry. Thin bark is shredding.
Habitat: Open woodlands, fields, dunes.
Comments: The berries are a favorite of cedar waxwings who were named for this tree.

BALDCYPRESS FAMILY

Large trees have thick, buttressed trunks and live up to 1000 years.

BALDCYPRESS
Taxodium distichum
Size: To 130 ft. (40 m)
Description: Distinguished at a glance by its flaring trunk. In water, protruding root 'knees' may be visible. Small rounded cones often hang in pairs.
Habitat: Swamps, along waterways.
Comments: Branches are often draped with the common southern air plant, Spanish moss. The wood is prized because it resists decay.

WAXMYRTLES & ALLIES

When the fruits of these trees are boiled in water, a waxy film rises to the surface that can be used to make candles. Five species occur in the U.S.

SOUTHERN WAXMYRTLE
Myrica cerifera
Size: To 30 ft. (9 m)
Description: Evergreen shrub or small tree has alternate, lance-shaped leaves spotted with resin that are broadest at the tip. Small gray-green fruits have a waxy coating.
Habitat: Wet sandy soils, swamps, pine and oak woodlands.
Comments: Fruits are a valuable source of food for birds. One of Florida's most widespread plants.

HICKORIES

Often grown as ornamentals, six species are native to Florida.

MOCKERNUT HICKORY
Carya tomentosa
Size: To 80 ft. (24 m)
Description: Leaves are up to 12 in. (30 cm) long and have 7-9 narrow, curved leaflets. Rounded, thick-shelled fruits have four prominent grooves. The kernels are sweet.
Habitat: Well-drained soils in northern Florida.
Comments: The strong, hard wood of this species is often used for firewood, furniture and ax handles.

BEECH FAMILY

Trees with smooth, light bark and nut-like fruits. Oaks are generally large trees with stout trunks and spreading crowns that produce acorns for fruit.

AMERICAN BEECH
Fagus grandifolia
Size: To 80 ft. (24 m)
Description: Straight trunk supports rounded crown. Alternate leaves are up to 6 in. long (15 cm) and sharp-toothed. Flowers bloom in rounded heads in spring and are succeeded by 3-sided nuts.
Habitat: Moist soils and well-drained lowlands in northern Florida.
Comments: Nuts are an important food source for squirrels and birds.

SOUTHERN RED OAK
Quercus falcata
Size: To 80 ft. (24 m)
Description: Large tree with a rounded crown. Leaves are deeply 3- to 7-lobed and are hairy beneath. Round acorn has cup enclosing about 1/3 of the nut.
Habitat: Poor upland soils, fertile bottomlands in northern Florida.
Comments: Also called Spanish oak, it is widely planted as a shade tree.

LIVE OAK
Quercus virginiana
Size: To 60 ft. (18 m)
Description: Tree has a spreading crown and is often wider than it is tall. Stiff leaves are leathery and have rolled edges. Dark acorns have a small cup that encloses about 1/4 of the nut.
Habitat: Sandy soils, hammocks, rich woods along waterways.
Comments: Trees occurring along the coast are often shrubby.

TURKEY OAK
Quercus laevis
Size: To 40 ft. (12 m)
Description: Small tree has irregular crown of crooked branches. Alternate leaves have 3-7 narrow lobes. Large, egg-shaped acorns have cups enclosing about 1/3 of the nut.
Habitat: Sandy hills, dry ridges in central and northern Florida.
Comments: Named for its leaves which resemble a turkey's foot.

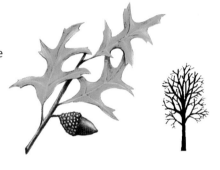

WATER OAK
Quercus nigra
Size: To 80 ft. (24 m)
Description: Wedge-shaped leaves are widest near the tip and to 5 in. (13 cm) long. Small, dark acorns have a shallow cup.
Habitat: Moist soils, swamps, common along waterways.
Comments: Often grows in association with sweetgum.

LAUREL OAK
Quercus laurifolia
Size: To 80 ft. (24 m)
Description: Shiny lance-shaped leaves are up to 5 in. (13 cm) long and have bristly edges. Shallow-cupped acorns are .5 in (1.3 cm) long.
Habitat: Well-drained, moist soils.
Comments: Widely planted as a shade tree throughout the southeast.

FIGS

Family of tropical plants produce fleshy fruits. Two species are native to North America, both of which are found only in Florida.

FLORIDA STRANGLER FIG
Ficus aurea
Size: To 70 ft. (21 m)
Description: Twisting trunk of young tree grows around the trunk of another tree. Alternate, evergreen leaves are leathery and 5 in. (13 cm) long. Fruits are small and rounded.
Habitat: Hammocks, coastal islands in southern Florida.
Comments: Seeds usually germinate in bark crevices of other trees and send out aerial roots that wrap around the host as they grow down to the soil. The strangler fig kills its host tree when it grows tall enough to shade it from sunlight. The less common shortleaf fig (*F. laevigata*) occurs in the Florida Keys.

BUCKWHEAT FAMILY

Large family of predominantly tropical trees and herbs has over 800 species.

SEAGRAPE
Coccoloba uvifera
Size: To 50 ft. (15 m)
Description: Tree or shrub has an open crown of spreading, often gnarled branches. Large, rounded leaves are wider than they are long. Purplish to greenish, grape-like fruits grow in long, hanging clusters.
Habitat: Common along beaches and shorelines.
Comments: Fruits are edible and best used for jelly. The similar dove plum (*C. diversifolia*) found in southeastern Florida has reddish, inedible fruits.

MAGNOLIAS

The trees in this family all have showy, fragrant flowers and are commonly planted as ornamentals.

SOUTHERN MAGNOLIA
Magnolia grandiflora
Size: To 100 ft. (30 m)
Description: Typically a large tree with a conical crown. Evergreen, glossy leaves are up to 10 in. (25 cm) long. Large creamy flowers (to 8 in./20 cm in diameter) have 9-14 petals. Cone-like, hairy fruits have bright red seeds.
Habitat: Rich woodlands, hammocks, along waterways.
Comments: The similar sweetbay (*M. virginiana*) has flowers 3 in. (8 cm) in diameter.

YELLOW POPLAR (TULIPTREE)
Liriodendron tulipifera
Size: To 120 ft. (36.5 m)
Description: Note unusual leaf shape. Showy flowers are succeeded by cone-like aggregates of papery, winged seeds. Large, greenish tulip-shaped flowers bloom in spring.
Habitat: Moist, well drained soils.
Comments: Is one of the most beautiful southern hardwoods.

LAURELS

Aromatic trees and shrubs provide camphor, cinnamon and scented oils.

RED BAY
Persea borbonia
Size: To 60 ft. (18 m)
Description: Lance-shaped, leathery leaves exude a spicy scent when crushed. Small clusters of yellowish spring flowers are succeeded by bluish berries.
Habitat: Wet valleys and swamps, mixed forests.
Comments: The leaves are used as a spice to flavor meats and soups. A handsome tree often planted as an ornamental.

WITCH-HAZEL FAMILY

Seven members of this subtropical family of trees and shrubs are native to North America.

SWEETGUM
Liquidambar styraciflua
Size: To 120 ft. (36.5 m)
Description: Large tree has spreading conical crown. Star-shaped leaves have 5-7 lobes and are 6 in. (15 cm) long. Small, greenish flowers bloom in tight, round clusters and are succeeded by hard, round fruits covered with woody spines. The fruits often persist into winter.
Habitat: Floodplains, moist valleys, mixed woodlands in central and northern Florida.
Comments: An important commercial species renowned for its tough, hard wood. The gummy, fragrant tree resin was once used to manufacture drugs and chewing gum.

PEAS & ALLIES

Most members of this large family of trees, shrubs and herbs produce fruit in seed pods.

SOUTHEASTERN CORALBEAN
Erythrina herbacea
Size: To 20 ft. (6 m)
Description: Shrub or small tree with crown of crooked, brittle branches. Roughly triangular leaves have slender stalks. Branches have stout, curved thorns. Distinctive, elongate scarlet flowers bloom in a showy spike and are succeeded by seed pods with red seeds.
Habitat: Sandy coastal areas, hammocks, pinelands.
Comments: Toxic seeds are sometimes used in jewelry. Some cultures use them to poison rodents and fish.

TORCHWOOD FAMILY

Tropical trees and shrubs have aromatic sap that has been used as a component of medicines and perfumes.

GUMBO-LIMBO
Bursera simarouba
Size: To 65 ft. (20 m)
Description: Red-brown bark peels off in sheets. Compound, leathery leaves are 8 in. (20 cm) long and have 3-9 leaflets. Whitish flowers bloom in dense clusters and are succeeded by football-shaped, 3-angled fruits.
Habitat: Hammocks and mixed forests in southern Florida.
Comments: Its turpentine-like resin has been used to manufacture glues, varnishes and medicines. Called tourist tree because its peeling red bark makes the tree look sunburned.

HOLLY FAMILY

Female plants of this group bear bright red berries in autumn.

AMERICAN HOLLY
Ilex opaca
Size: To 70 ft. (21 m)
Description: Tree is distinguished by its stiff, spiny, evergreen leaves. Greenish-white flowers are succeeded by bright red berries.
Habitat: Moist bottomlands, coastal.
Comments: One of 5 hollies native to Florida.

YAUPON
Ilex vomitoria
Size: To 20 ft. (6 m)
Description: Bushy shrub or tree with short trunk. Alternate, evergreen leaves have wavy-toothed edges. Flowers bloom in small clusters and are succeeded by red, berry-like fruits that persist into winter.
Habitat: Swamps, along waterways in central and northern Florida.
Comments: The similar dahoon (*I. cassine*) has leaves lacking wavy edges. It is found throughout Florida.

MAPLES

Maples are distinguished by their large leaves and winged seed pairs.

RED MAPLE
Acer rubrum
Size: To 90 ft. (27 m)
Description: Tree has a large crown of spreading branches. Leaves have 3-5 lobes and turn scarlet in autumn. Reddish flowers bloom in drooping clusters and are succeeded by red, winged seed pairs (samaras).
Habitat: Moist soils in a variety of habitats.
Comments: A fast-growing species often planted as a shade tree in cities.

MANGROVES

Evergreen trees and shrubs often form dense thickets in coastal areas.

RED MANGROVE
Rhizophora mangle
Size: To 80 ft. (24 m)
Description: Easily distinguished by its numerous arching prop roots. Torpedo-shaped seedlings grow out of egg-shaped fruits.
Habitat: Coastal swamps and estuaries in southern Florida.
Comments: One of 3 species of mangrove native to Florida. All are important because they prevent erosion along shorelines and their roots serve as nurseries for mollusks and fish.

MYRSINE FAMILY

Two members of this tropical family are native to Florida.

MARLBERRY
Ardisia escallonioides
Size: To 25 ft. (7.6 m)
Description: Evergreen, alternate leaves are leathery and dotted with dark glands. Whitish flowers bloom in branching clusters and are succeeded by shiny brown-black fruits.
Habitat: Variable, often in the shade of other trees.
Comments: Common throughout southern Florida.

PERSIMMONS

Members of the ebony family, persimmons have black heartwood.

COMMON PERSIMMON
Diospyros virginiana
Size: To 60 ft. (18 m)
Description: Tree has a rounded crown of stout branches. Oval, leathery leaves are shiny above. Small whitish flowers bloom near the base of the leaf stalks and are succeeded by round orange to purple fruits.
Habitat: Moist bottomlands, fields.
Comments: The fleshy fruits are a valuable food source for wildlife.

INTRODUCED EXOTICS

These introduced trees have spread widely throughout parts of Florida and are considered 'bad exotics' by many because they take over habitats occupied by native species.

BRAZILIAN PEPPER
Schinus terebinthifolius
Size: To 50 ft. (15 m)
Description: Shrub or tree has a rounded crown. Alternate, evergreen compound leaves have up to 13 leaflets. Elongate clusters of yellowish flowers are succeeded by red berries.
Habitat: Variable.
Comments: Also called Florida holly.

AUSTRALIAN PINE
Casuarina equisitifolia
Size: To 100 ft. (30 m)
Description: Straight-trunked tree has conical crown. Long, drooping branchlets are composed of small, jointed twigs. Small, cone-like fruits are less than 1 in. (2.5 cm) in diameter.
Habitat: Sandy soils, along seashores.
Comments: This controversial species was introduced for erosion control and has since spread quickly, crowding out native species in many areas. Not a true pine, it is one of 3 similar species growing in Florida.

CHINESE TALLOW
Sapium sebiferum
Size: To 30 ft. (9 m)
Description: Alternate leaves are widest near the base and have long stems. Brown fruits split open in fall, revealing 3 white seeds that cling together in a ball and remain attached to the branchlet.
Habitat: Sandy soils, near streams.
Comments: The leaves of this popular ornamental turn red in the fall. Milky sap is poisonous. Also called popcorn tree.

PUNK TREE
Melaleuca quinquenervia
Size: To 50 ft. (15 m)
Description: Trunk and branches have shredding bark. Stiff leaves are pointed at both ends and smell spicy when crushed. Whitish flowers bloom in showy 'bottlebrush' clusters and are succeeded by small rounded fruits.
Habitat: Wet bottomlands, swamps.
Comments: Introduced to dry out parts of the Everglades, this fast-growing Australian species absorbs water like a sponge.

LILY & PALM FAMILIES

Both of these families belong to the group of angiosperms called monocots. Most have parallel-veined leaves and trunks that lack annual growth rings. Eight of the 14 palms native to the U.S. are found in Florida.

Florida's State Tree

CABBAGE PALM
Sabal palmetto
Size: To 80 ft. (24 m)
Description: Slender tree has large fan-shaped leaves with blades to 6.5 ft. (2 m) long. Large hanging clusters of yellowish flowers are succeeded by black, berry-like fruits.
Habitat: Marshes, woodlands, hammocks, sea coasts.
Comments: Named for its edible sprout core that can be eaten like cabbage.

FLORIDA ROYAL PALM
Roystonea elata
Size: To 120 ft. (36.5 m)
Description: Beautiful palm is easily distinguished by the smooth green leaf sheath near the top of the trunk.
Habitat: Hammocks, rich soils.
Comments: The introduced Manila palm (*Veitchia merrillii*) is similar but smaller (to 20 ft./6 m).

SAW PALMETTO
Serenoa repens
Size: To 25 ft. (7.6 m)
Description: Usually a low shrubby palm with a buried trunk; sometimes upright and tree-like. Leaves have stems with saw-toothed edges.
Habitat: Hammocks, roadsides, scrub land, sand dunes.
Comments: Likely the most common native plant throughout Florida.

COCONUT PALM
Cocos nucifera
Size: To 100 ft. (30 m)
Description: This classic desert-island palm is told by its smooth, often curved, trunk and large crown of feathery leaves. The familiar fruit is a fibrous nut 10-12 in. (25-30 cm) long.
Habitat: Coastal.
Comments: A widespread non-native species in southern Florida.

WASHINGTONIA
Washingtonia spp.
Size: To 60 ft. (18 m)
Description: Told at a glance by its crown of large, fan-shaped leaves and the shaggy sack of dead leaves hanging beneath it.
Habitat: Moist soils.
Comments: Native to the southwestern U.S., it is planted along streets throughout southern Florida.

WHAT ARE WILDFLOWERS?

Wildflowers are soft-stemmed flowering plants, usually smaller than trees or shrubs, that grow anew each year. Some regenerate annually from the same rootstock (perennials), while others grow from seeds and last a single season (annuals). Most have flowering stems bearing colorful blossoms which ripen into fruits as the growing season progresses. The flowering stem typically grows upright, but may be climbing, creeping or trailing.

N.B. *– This section covers wildflowers and includes some shrubs that are conspicuous when in bloom.*

The species in this section have been grouped according to color rather than family to facilitate field identification. The color groups used are:

- White
- Yellow, Orange and Green
- Red and Pink
- Blue and Purple

HOW TO IDENTIFY WILDFLOWERS

After noting color, examine the shape of the flower heads. Are they daisy-like, bell-shaped, or cross-shaped? How are they arranged on the plant? Do they occur singly or in clusters? Are the flower heads upright or drooping? Pay close attention to the leaves and how they are arranged on the stem. Refer to the illustrations and text to confirm its size, habitat and blooming period.

N.B. *– The blooming periods of flowers can vary depending on latitude, elevation and the weather. The dates given are meant to serve as general guidelines only.*

Remember that flowers are wildlife and should be treated as such. Many species have been seriously depleted due to loss of habitat and overpicking. In many areas, once-abundant species are now rare. Bring along a sketchbook and camera to record the flowers you see instead of picking them. This will help ensure there are more blossoms for you and others to enjoy in years to come.

FLOWER STRUCTURE

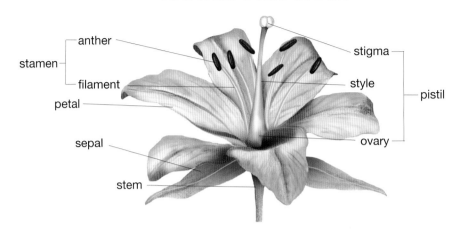

FLOWER SHAPES

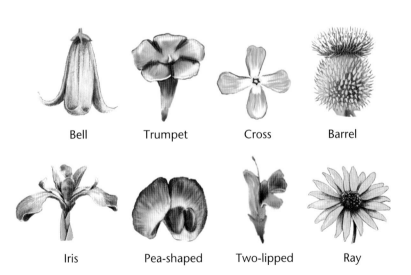

Bell

Trumpet

Cross

Barrel

Iris

Pea-shaped

Two-lipped

Ray

WHITE FLOWERS

MOONFLOWER
Ipomoea alba
Size: To 7 ft. (2.1 m)
Description: Climbing vine has heart-shaped to oval leaves. Large, white bell-shaped flowers (to 5 in./13 cm wide) bloom at night throughout the year.
Habitat: Beaches, roadsides, hammocks, waste areas.
Comments: Fragrant blossoms are pollinated at night by moths.

STRING LILY
Crinum americanum
Size: To 3 ft. (90 cm)
Description: Delicate, star-like white flowers have 6 slender petal-like segments; they bloom in clusters of 3-6 from May to September. Slender basal leaves are slightly toothed.
Habitat: Swamps, marshes, wet forests.
Comments: Also called swamp lily, it is frequently cultivated by gardeners.

BEGGARTICK
Bidens alba
Size: To 4 in. (10 cm)
Description: White, notched flower rays surround a bright yellow disk.
Habitat: Disturbed and waste areas.
Comments: Produces barbed fruits that stick to people and animals. Blooms year-round.

FRAGRANT WATER LILY
Nymphaea odorata
Size: Flower to 6 in. (15 cm) wide.
Description: Common aquatic plant is distinguished by its large, many-rayed, white to pinkish, yellow-centered flowers. Round leafpads are notched at their base. Blooms nearly year-round.
Habitat: Ponds, lakes, streams.
Comments: This floating plant is rooted to the bottom and usually grows in water less than 8 ft. (2.4 m) deep.

ARROWHEAD
Sagittaria latifolia
Size: To 3 ft. (90 cm)
Description: Small, white 3-petalled flowers bloom atop rigid stems in whorls of 3. Basal leaves are arrowhead-shaped. Blooms July-October.
Habitat: Ponds, slow streams, marshes, ditches.
Comments: The plant produces underground tubers that were an important food source for early settlers. Also called Wapato.

JIMSONWEED
Datura stramonium
Size: To 6 ft. (1.8 m)
Description: White to lavender trumpet-shaped flowers to 4 in. (10 cm) long bloom June-October. Oval, alternate leaves are coarsely toothed. Flowers are succeeded by round, prickly fruits.
Habitat: Fields, waste areas.
Comments: All parts of the plant are poisonous.

ATAMASCO LILY
Zephyranthes atamasco
Size: To 12 in. (30 cm)
Description: White lily-like flowers are often tinged with pink. Grass-like leaves have sharp edges.
Habitat: Pine flatwoods, meadows.
Comments: This flower usually blooms around Easter and is also called Easter lily.

QUEEN ANNE'S LACE
Daucus carota
Size: To 4 ft. (1.2 m)
Description: Distinguished by large, flat-topped flowers clusters and lacy foliage. The flower clusters become cup-shaped as they age.
Habitat: Roadsides, waste areas.
Comments: Introduced species is a relative of the garden carrot. The plant closely resembles the toxic poison hemlock.

ALOE YUCCA
Yucca aloifolia
Size: To 15 ft. (4.5 m)
Description: Plant may or may not be tree-like. Stiff, sharp-pointed leaves are up to 3 ft. (90 cm) long. Creamy, cup-shaped white flowers bloom in a long terminal spike and are fragrant at night.
Habitat: Sand dunes, coastal marshes.
Comments: Also called Spanish bayonet, it is commonly planted as an ornamental. The flowers are pollinated primarily by the yucca moth, a nocturnal species.

WHITE SWEET CLOVER
Melilotus alba
Size: To 7 ft. (2.1 m)
Description: Tall leafy plant has long spikes of tiny, white, pea-shaped flowers. Alternate leaves have 3 leaflets notched at the tip. Blooms May-October.
Habitat: Roadsides, lawns, waste areas, fields.
Comments: Non-native species was originally imported with lawn grasses. Flowers have the scent of hay.

INDIAN PIPE
Monotropa uniflora
Size: To 12 in. (30 cm)
Description: Waxy, white plant has several stems supporting a single, nodding, cup-shaped, white to pinkish flower. The entire plant darkens in color with age.
Habitat: Deciduous woods and shady places in central and northern Florida.
Comments: It lacks the pigment chlorophyll necessary for photosynthesis and obtains nourishment from living and decaying plants.

TREAD SOFTLY
Cnidoscolus stimulosus
Size: To 3 ft. (90 cm)
Description: Entire plant is covered with stiff, stinging hairs. Alternate leaves are heart-shaped and 3-5 lobed. White flowers have 5 petal-like lobes and bloom year-round.
Habitat: Pinelands, sandhills, beaches, disturbed areas.
Comments: Also called spurge nettle.

SWAMP ROSE MALLOW
Hibiscus moscheutos
Size: To 8 ft. (2.4 m)
Description: Large rose-like flowers (to 8 in./20 cm across) have petals that are pinkish on their inner edge. Style is very long. Blooms June-September.
Habitat: Swamps, floodplains, wet areas in northern Florida.
Comments: One of several species of hibiscus found in Florida.

GOPHER APPLE
Licania michauxii
Size: To 12 in. (30 cm)
Description: Evergreen plant produces a cluster of delicate white flowers. Small red fruits are apple-like.
Habitat: Roadsides, sandhills, oak woodlands.
Comments: Also called ground oak, its thin veined leaves are oak-like. Fruit is a valuable source of food for wildlife.

MUSKY MINT
Hyptis alata
Size: To 7 ft. (2.1 m)
Description: Opposite, lance-shaped leaves are strongly toothed and woolly underneath. Creamy flowers bloom in puffy terminal clusters throughout the year.
Habitat: Low, moist areas, pinelands, hammocks.
Comments: Three similar species of *Hyptis* are found in Florida.

BUTTONBUSH
Cephalanthus occidentalis
Size: To 10 ft. (3 m)
Description: Shiny, opposite or whorled leaves are oval-shaped and dark green. 'Pincushion' flowers have protruding stamens.
Habitat: Margins of swamps, ponds and waterways.
Comments: The fragrant flowers attract a number of insect pollinators including bees.

LAMB'S QUARTERS
Chenopodium album
Size: To 6 ft. (1.8 m)
Description: Erect plant is covered with a mealy substance when young. Small, cauliflower-like white to pinkish flowers bloom in dense clusters June-October.
Habitat: Disturbed areas, roadsides, streets, lawns.
Comments: Related to spinach, the leaves of young plants are edible and high in vitamins. Also called pigweed.

LIZARD'S TAIL
Saururus cernuus
Size: To 5 ft. (1.5 m)
Description: Leaves are arrow- or heart-shaped. Flowers bloom in a nodding terminal cluster up to 12 in. (30 cm) long.
Habitat: Wet woods, marshes, along streams.
Comments: Plant forms extensive colonies.

WHITE CLOVER
Trifolium repens
Size: Stems to 10 in. (25 cm)
Description: Long-stemmed, dark green leaves have three oval leaflets. Rounded white flowers bloom April-September.
Habitat: Fields, lawns waste areas.
Comments: The common lawn clover, it is an excellent nectar producer and a favorite of bees. Red clover (*T. pratense*) is also found in Florida.

YELLOW, ORANGE & GREEN FLOWERS

BUTTERFLYWEED
Asclepias tuberosa
Size: To 3 ft. (90 cm)
Description: Bright orange, star-like flowers bloom in large clusters May-September. Stem may be erect or crawling. Alternate leaves are lance-shaped.
Habitat: Meadows, fields, roadsides, prairies.
Comments: Unlike other milkweed species, it lacks milky sap. As its name suggests, it is a favorite of butterflies.

STICK-TIGHT
Bidens laevis
Size: To 3 ft. (90 cm)
Description: Bright yellow flowers have 6-8 rays surrounding a large, dark disk. Narrow leaves are usually toothed. Blooms nearly throughout the year.
Habitat: Swamps, meadows, along waterways.
Comments: A member of the sticktight family, it has small, barbed fruits that cling to clothing and fur.

COMMON EVENING PRIMROSE
Oenothera biennis
Size: To 5 ft. (1.5 m)
Description: Pale yellow, 4-petalled, flowers bloom in clusters atop a leafy red-purple stem. Lemon-scented flowers bloom June-September.
Habitat: Roadsides, open, disturbed areas.
Comments: The flowers bloom in the evening and stay open overnight. At least 8 similar species of evening primroses found in Florida.

SUNFLOWER
Helianthus **spp.**
Size: To 10 ft. (3 m)
Description: Tall, leafy plant with a branching stem supporting numerous yellow, dark-centered flowers. Blooms June-September.
Habitat: Roadsides, disturbed areas, open fields.
Comments: Flowers follow the sun across the sky each day. Over 15 species of *Helianthus* are found in Florida.

YELLOW JESSAMINE
Gelsemium sempervirens
Size: Vine to 20 ft. (6 m) long
Description: Vine has clusters of trumpet-shaped, fragrant yellow flowers.
Habitat: Dry woodlands, sandy areas.
Comments: Common along roadsides. All parts of the plant are poisonous and contain an alkaloid similar to strychnine.

HOODED PITCHER PLANT
Sarracenia minor
Size: To 2 ft. (60 cm)
Description: Large, erect leaves are hooded and dark-veined near the top. Yellow, 5-petalled flowers bloom April-July; the leaves last into autumn.
Habitat: Bogs, wet pinelands.
Comments: The most common of 6 species of pitcher plants found on wet, acidic soils in northern Florida. All trap insects which are digested by the plant.

CENTURY PLANT
Agave **spp.**
Size: To 14 ft. (4.2 m)
Description: Tall, candelabra-like flowering stalk rises from a rosette of gray-green leaves. Yellow flowers bloom in dense clusters during summer months.
Habitat: Tropical south Florida.
Comments: Plant takes several years to flower and blooms only once. Often planted as an ornamental in cities.

BLACK-EYED SUSAN
Rudbeckia hirta
Size: To 3 ft. (90 cm)
Description: Flowers have long yellow rays (often drooping) surrounding a brown, cone-shaped central disk.
Habitat: Waste areas, fields.
Comments: Stems and leaves are bristly to the touch.

YELLOW BACHELOR'S BUTTON
Polygala lutea
Size: To 12 in. (30 cm)
Description: Bright, rounded, orange-yellow flowers bloom at end of branching stems throughout most of the year.
Habitat: Pinelands, moist soils.
Comments: A member of the milkwort family, some species of which it was once believed could increase the flow of milk if fed to livestock and mothers.

PARTRIDGE PEA
Cassia chamaecrista
Size: To 30 in. (75 cm)
Description: Bright yellow flowers have 5 petals with purplish to brown centers. Alternate leaves have up to 18 pairs of narrow leaflets. Blooms throughout the year.
Habitat: Pinelands, flatwoods, roadsides, disturbed areas.
Comments: The similar wild senna (*C. marilandica*) has leaves with 4-8 pairs of oval leaflets.

ATLANTIC ST. JOHN'S WORT
Hypericum reductum
Size: To 2 ft. (60 cm)
Description: Evergreen shrub has bright canary-yellow flowers. Needle-like leaves grow in whorls along the stem. Stems are red-brown.
Habitat: Wet and dry areas with well-drained soils.
Comments: Drought-tolerant shrub grows up to 3 ft. (90 cm) wide.

YELLOW POND LILY
Nuphar lutea
Size: Flower to 3 in. (8 cm) wide.
Description: Aquatic plant has large heart-shaped leaves with long stalks. Cup-shaped, bulbous yellow flowers bloom May-October.
Habitat: Ponds and sluggish streams.
Comments: Widely used by Native Americans for food, the roots were eaten boiled or roasted and the seeds popped like popcorn.

COMMON MULLEIN
Verbascum thapsus
Size: To 7 ft. (2.1 m)
Description: Tall leafy plant that tapers from a broad base to a slender spike of yellow flowers. Flowers bloom a few at a time throughout summer.
Habitat: Roadsides, fields and waste areas.
Comments: Common roadside weed was once used to create torches by dipping the stalk in tallow. Non-native.

SNEEZEWEED
Helenium amarum
Size: To 20 in. (50 cm)
Description: Leaves are long and thread-like and flowering stems are grooved. Drooping, yellow petal-like structures bloom at the base of a large flower head May-October.
Habitat: Disturbed sites, sandy soils, roadsides.
Comments: A member of the sneezeweed family, the dried leaves can induce violent sneezing if inhaled.

COMMON PLANTAIN
Plantago major
Size: To 20 in. (50 cm)
Description: Large, tough basal leaves are finely-toothed with deep longitudinal veins. Tiny greenish flowers bloom in a slender spike.
Habitat: Very common in lawns, gardens and waste areas.
Comments: An introduced weed widespread throughout the country.

YELLOW BUTTONS
Balduina angustifolium
Size: To 3 ft. (90 cm)
Description: Erect plant has narrow, alternate leaves. Distinctive flower has 3-lobed rays and a large 'honeycombed' central disk. Blooms year round.
Habitat: Pinelands, scrub areas.
Comments: Common throughout Florida.

SPANISH MOSS
Tillandsia usneoides
Size: To 25 ft. (7.6 m)
Description: Grayish stringy plant hangs in clumps from tree limbs. Tiny yellowish flowers are rarely seen.
Habitat: Trees, poles in hammocks, oak and pine woodlands.
Comments: This very common air plant is often seen draping the limbs of baldcypresses, live oaks and other trees in moist areas.

PRICKLY PEAR CACTUS
Opuntia spp.
Size: Pads to 12 in. (30 cm)
Description: A sprawling or erect cactus with jointed, prickly pads. Red-centered, yellow flowers bloom April-June.
Habitat: Dry areas.
Comments: Both the fruit and the pads are consumed by wildlife and humans.

LOTUS LILY
Nelumbo lutea
Size: Flowers to 10 in. (25 cm) wide.
Description: Stout stalks support leaves and flowers above the water. Huge leaves are up to 2 ft. (60 cm) wide. Large yellow flowers to 8 in. (20 cm) wide bloom July-October.
Habitat: Still fresh water.
Comments: The center of the flower is a salt-shaker like structure that persists long after the petals have fallen off. The pink sacred lotus (*N. nucifera*) is also found in Florida.

GIANT AIR PLANT
Tillandsia fasciculata
Size: To 2 ft. (60 cm)
Description: Usually found growing on trees, it has a whorl of stiff elongate leaves. Small flowers bloom within a showy red and yellow flower-like spike January-August.
Habitat: Cypress swamps, hammocks.
Comments: A non-parasitic air plant, it feeds on nutrients obtained from the air, rain and its host's bark.

FLORIDA BUTTERFLY ORCHID
Encyclia tampensis
Size: To 2 ft. (60 cm)
Description: Yellow-green flowers have a white lowermost petal tinged with maroon or brown.
Habitat: Swamps.
Comments: Plant usually grows in loose hanging clusters on palms and other trees.

COMMON CATTAIL
Typha latifolia
Size: To 10 ft. (3 m)
Description: Distinguished by its prominent club-like sheath of greenish flower spikes atop a long stalk. The flowers ripen into brownish tufts of hairy seeds in late summer.
Habitat: Common in marshes, ditches and along lakes and rivers.
Comments: Cattails provide a vital source of food and cover for water birds and wildlife.

TICKSEED
Coreopsis lanceolata
Size: To 2 ft. (60 cm)
Description: Slender, lance-shaped leaves are primarily basal. Slender stems support solitary, daisy-like yellow flowers with notched rays. Blooms May-August.
Habitat: Waste areas, roadsides, fields.
Comments: One of a number of tickseeds found in Florida.

RED & PINK FLOWERS

TRUMPET HONEYSUCKLE
Lonicera sempervirens
Size: Vine to 10 ft. (3 m)
Description: Distinguished at
a glance by its yellow-throated,
trumpet-shaped red flowers.
Blooms March-September. A pair
of leaves are often fused together
below the flower cluster.
Habitat: Woods, thickets.
Comments: Flowers produce a
sweet nectar that attracts butterflies
and hummingbirds.

LANTANA
Lantana camara
Size: To 40 in. (1 m)
Description: Shrub has distinctive
rounded clusters of 5-petalled flowers
arranged in an inner and outer
ring of differing colors. Opposite,
heart-shaped leaves are toothed.
Blooms throughout the year.
Habitat: Roadsides, waste areas,
open woods.
Comments: The flowers may be
orange, yellow, pink or white. Entire
plant has a strong odor. Non-native
invasive.

WILD POINSETTIA
Euphorbia heterophylla
Size: To 3 ft. (90 cm)
Description: Small, rounded,
greenish flowers bloom amid showy
red bracts throughout most of the
year. Large leaves are often blotched
with red.
Habitat: Pinelands, moist, sandy soils
and clearings.
Comments: Closely related to the
introduced, commercial Christmas
poinsettia (*E. pulcherrima*) that is
often found in waste areas but is
not naturalized.

TROPICAL SAGE
Salvia coccinea
Size: To 2 ft. (60 cm)
Description: Heart-shaped leaves have scalloped edges. Bright red tubular flowers have a drooping lower lip. Flowers bloom in whorls along the stem.
Habitat: Hammocks, roadsides.
Comments: The leaves are the best way to distinguish this plant from the similar cardinal flower.

GRASS-PINK ORCHID
Calopogon spp.
Size: To 20 in. (50 cm)
Description: Fragrant pink to purplish flowers bloom in a loose cluster atop a leafless stem. Single basal leaf is grass-like.
Habitat: Swamps, bogs, wet meadows.
Comments: These orchids are tolerant of a wide variety of nutrient poor, acidic soils. They bloom May-August.

BUTTERFLY PEA
Centrosema virginianum
Size: Vine to 4 ft. (1.2 m) long.
Description: Easily distinguished by its showy, pink to lavender, upside-down flowers with a small spur near the base on the back. Alternate leaves are divided into 3 lance-shaped leaflets. Blooms year-round.
Habitat: Open woods, dry, sandy areas, fields.
Comments: One of a number of similar species of pea found in Florida.

PINE LILY
Lilium catesbaei
Size: To 3 ft. (90 cm)
Description: Striking red-orange plant has dark-spotted, recurved petals that are yellow at the base. Alternate, stalkless leaves grow scattered along the stem. Blooms July-September.
Habitat: Swamps, pinelands, wet woods, bogs.
Comments: Also called southern red lily, it is an endangered species.

FIREWHEEL
Gaillardia pulchella
Size: To 2 ft. (60 cm)
Description: Fiery pinwheel-shaped flowers have red rays often tipped in yellow. Inner disk is maroon and dome-shaped. Blooms throughout the year.
Habitat: Sandy soils, disturbed areas, roadsides, beaches.
Comments: Conspicuous along roadsides, they often blanket large open areas.

CARDINAL FLOWER
Lobelia cardinalis
Size: To 3 ft. (90 cm)
Description: Plant with spike of striking, red tubular flowers. Lance-shaped leaves have toothed edges. Blooms June-October.
Habitat: Wet areas, along waterways.
Comments: Also called scarlet lobelia, its flowers are a favorite of hummingbirds.

PINK PURSLANE
Portulaca pilosa
Size: To 8 in. (20 cm)
Description: Prostrate to erect plant has 5-petaled pink flowers with prominent yellow stamens. Fleshy leaves are succulent in appearance.
Habitat: Dry, sandy soils.
Comments: Flowers bloom throughout the year. Common names include hairy pigweed and kiss-me-quick.

SWAMP MILKWEED
Asclepias incarnata
Size: To 5 ft. (1.5 m)
Description: Small pink, star-shaped flowers bloom in large terminal clusters throughout most of the year. Leaves are lance-shaped and grow in pairs.
Habitat: Moist areas, wet woods.
Comments: Named for its milky sap, its leaves are poisonous to all but a few animals. The monarch butterfly eats only milkweed leaves and is subsequently toxic to most of its predators.

COMMON FLEABANE
Erigeron spp.
Size: To 3 ft. (90 cm)
Description: Erect plant supports small pink to white ray flowers (1 in./3 cm wide) on a branching stem. Blooms March-October.
Habitat: Meadows, open woods.
Comments: One of several fleabanes found in Florida. The plants were once hung in houses to keep fleas away.

LADY'S THUMB
Polygonum persicaria
Size: To 40 in. (1 m)
Description: Small pink flowers bloom in dense terminal spikes atop pink stems June-October. Narrow leaves have a dark mark in the middle.
Habitat: Roadsides, disturbed areas in southern Florida.
Comments: The dark leaf-spot is thought to resemble a lady's thumbprint.

SKYROCKET
Ipomopsis spp.
Size: To 6 ft. (1.8 m)
Description: Slender stems support clusters of bright red, tubular flowers resembling exploded fireworks. Blooms May-September.
Habitat: Open woodlands, dry hillsides, sandy areas.
Comments: Common in Florida's orange groves. Also known as Spanish larkspur.

BLAZING STAR
Liatris spicata
Size: To 5 ft. (1.5 m)
Description: Distinguished by its spike of feathery, red-purplish flowers with protruding styles. Alternate leaves grow crowded along stem length. Blooms July-November.
Habitat: Moist woods, wet fields.
Comments: Also called gayfeather, it is one of several *Liatris* species found in Florida.

PINK SUNDEW
Drosera capillaris
Size: To 8 in. (20 cm)
Description: Basal leaves are covered with reddish, sticky droplets. White-to-pink, 5-petaled flowers bloom in a terminal cluster June-September.
Habitat: Bogs, wet woods.
Comments: A carnivorous plant that feeds on the bugs that are attracted to, and entrapped by, the sweet, sticky fluid excreted by its leaves.

MEADOW BEAUTY
Rhexia mariana
Size: To 2 ft. (60 cm)
Description: Flowers have 4 lopsided pink to whitish petals. Central disk has 8 prominent stamens. Square stem has two sides of different widths.
Habitat: Moist open areas.
Comments: The unusual fruits of this plant were aptly described by Thoreau as "perfect little cream pitchers".

ROSE MALLOW
Hibiscus coccineus
Size: To 10 ft. (3 m)
Description: Distinguished as a large, leafy plant with stunning crimson flowers. Toothed leaves are divided into narrow segments. Blooms June-September.
Habitat: Swamps, tidal marshes.
Comments: Popular ornamental is often cultivated.

FERN ROSE
Kosteletzkya virginica
Size: To 3 ft. (90 cm)
Description: Large plant has showy, pink, 5-petaled flowers with yellow stamens forming a column around the style.
Habitat: Salt- and freshwater marshes and ditches.
Comments: Like its hibiscus relatives, it is often grown as an ornamental.

BLUE & PURPLE FLOWERS

VERVAIN
Verbena **spp.**
Size: To 5 ft. (1.5 m)
Description: Small blue to lavender flowers grow in rings around tall candelabra-like flowering spikes. Blooms June-September.
Habitat: Fields, roadsides, along waterways.
Comments: One of over 10 Florida vervains, they range in color from white to blue. Many cultures feel vervains have sacred, healing powers, and have used them to treat a variety of ailments since ancient times.

PICKERELWEED
Pontederia cordata
Size: To 4 ft. (1.2 m)
Description: Aquatic plant has heart-shaped to oval leaves. Bright blue flowers bloom in a dense spike May-November. Each flower has 2 yellow spots on its central upper petal.
Habitat: Ditches, shorelines, swamps, streams.
Comments: Usually grows in shallow water. Seeds and young leaf stalks are edible.

MISTFLOWER
Conoclinium coelestinum
Size: To 6 ft. (1.8 m)
Description: Dense clusters of blue-violet, fuzzy flowers bloom atop sprawling stems June-October. Opposite leaves are arrowhead-shaped.
Habitat: Wet woods, meadows, along streams.
Comments: Also called blue boneset, it is one of several similar species found in Florida.

SLENDER DAYFLOWER
Commelina erecta
Size: To 3 ft. (90 cm)
Description: Sprawling plant has upright stems supporting striking flowers with two large, rounded blue upper petals and a small white lower petal. Blooms May-October.
Habitat: Pinelands, scrub areas in central and southern Florida.
Comments: Named for its short-lived blossoms. Introduced from Asia.

CAROLINA WILD PETUNIA
Ruellia caroliniensis
Size: To 3 ft. (90 cm)
Description: Violet, trumpet-shaped flowers have 5 petals. Leaves are elliptical to oval.
Habitat: Open woods, pinelands.
Comments: The flowers are reminiscent of garden petunias.

ASTER
Aster **spp.**
Size: To 3 ft. (90 cm)
Description: Distinguished by its purplish to pinkish, yellow-centered flowers with broad rays. Blooms July-October.
Habitat: Meadows, forests, roadsides, fields.
Comments: One of several species of aster found in Florida. All have the familiar starburst flower heads and are usually purplish or blue.

BLUE-EYED GRASS
Sisyrinchium atlanticum
Size: To 2 ft. (60 cm)
Description: Slender stems support one or more delicate, 6-petalled, star-shaped blue-violet flowers. Blooms March-September.
Habitat: Hammocks, bogs, flatwoods.
Comments: Yellow and white variants of blue-eyed grass are also found in Florida.

JOE-PYE-WEED
Eupatorium **spp.**
Size: To 7 ft. (2.1 m)
Description: A large, domed cluster of fuzzy, pink-purple flowers bloom atop a tall, hollow stem July-September. Narrow leaves grow in whorls of 3-5 along the stem.
Habitat: Fields, ditches, damp areas.
Comments: The leaves smell like vanilla when crushed. Plant is named after a Native American doctor who used the plant to cure many ills.

IRIS
Iris **spp.**
Size: To 25 in. (63 cm)
Description: Slender stalks support distinctive, large blue to white flowers. Petals often have a central yellow-orange stripe and purple veins. Grass-like basal leaves arch away from the plant and may lie on the ground. Blooms in spring.
Habitat: Swamps, marshes, wet shores, along waterways.
Comments: Five species of iris, often called blue flag, are found in Florida.

BLUE TOADFLAX
Nuttallanthus canadensis
Size: To 28 in. (70 cm)
Description: Upright blue-green plant has alternate, narrow leaves growing along the entire stem. Bluish, two-lipped, spurred flowers bloom in a long terminal cluster May-September.
Habitat: Roadsides, disturbed areas, sandy soils.
Comments: A native plant that has become widespread throughout North America, it is also called old-field toadflax. A member of the snapdragon family

WATER HYACINTH
Eichhornia crassipes
Size: To 3 ft. (90 cm)
Description: Floating plant is supported by inflated stalks. Showy spikes of purple flowers bloom throughout the year. Each flower has a yellow 'eye' on the central upper petal.
Habitat: Rivers, ponds, waterways, ditches.
Comments: This introduced nuisance plant spreads quickly and chokes warm waterways throughout the south. Manatees are one of the few creatures that feed on it.

PASSIONFLOWER
Passiflora incarnata
Size: Climbing vine to 20 ft. (6 m) high.
Description: Lavender flower (to 4 in./10 cm wide) has a showy fringe of tendrils. Alternate leaves have 3 lobes. Blooms May-October.
Habitat: Thickets, fields, roadsides.
Comments: Also called maypop, it is a key food source for a number of larval butterflies.

CHICORY
Cichorium intybus
Size: To 6 ft. (1.8 m)
Description: Wheel-shaped, pale blue flowers bloom atop slender branching stems April-October.
Habitat: Fields, roadsides, waste areas.
Comments: The roots are used as a coffee substitute.

SEA LAVENDER
Limonium carolinianum
Size: To 2 ft. (60 cm)
Description: Lavender-to-pink flowers blossom in arching clusters at the end of wiry stems. Basal leaves are typically spoon-shaped.
Habitat: Coastal areas including mangrove swamps and brackish marshes.
Comments: Dense colonies cover coastal marshlands in summer.

FLORIDA REGIONS

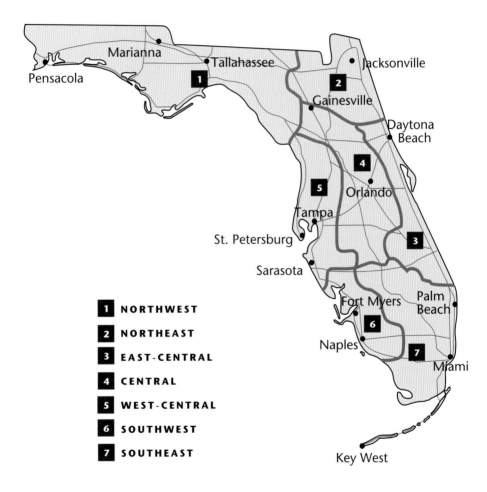

Marianna
Tallahassee
Pensacola
1
Jacksonville
2
Gainesville
Daytona
Beach
4
5
Orlando
Tampa
St. Petersburg
3
Sarasota
Fort Myers
Palm
Beach
6
Naples
7
Miami
Key West

1 NORTHWEST

2 NORTHEAST

3 EAST-CENTRAL

4 CENTRAL

5 WEST-CENTRAL

6 SOUTHWEST

7 SOUTHEAST

1 NORTHWEST

The panhandle is a temperate region characterized by rolling hills and extensive longleaf pine forests. The area is geologically older than the rest of the state and the site of the highest point in Florida. The land is dissected by some of the state's largest rivers including the Apalachicola, Choctawhatchee and Escambia. The Florida canyon lands are a testament to the area's ancestral rivers. The coastal area is noted for its abundant wildlife and nature preserves.

2 NORTHEAST

Sand dunes, marshes, cypress swamps, wetlands, prairies and pine woodlands are a few of the regional habitats that support a rich array of flora and fauna. The Osceola National Forest encompasses vast swamps and wetlands that support a number of endangered species. The beaches and islands along the Atlantic coast attract thousands of nesting shore and sea birds in summer, and the interior prairie hosts up to 2,000 sandhill cranes in winter.

3 EAST-CENTRAL

This extensively developed area encompasses a number of important refuges that provide critical wildlife habitats. The Merritt National Wildlife Refuge provides sanctuary for up to 200,000 wintering waterfowl.

4 CENTRAL

This region is characterized by expansive scrub forests, and numerous warm springs and rivers. The northern area is dominated by the sand pine scrub woodlands of the Ocala National Forest. The southern lake country encompasses habitats harboring dozens of species of endangered and threatened plants and animals including rare snail kites and whooping cranes. The region is also home to the largest nesting population of bald eagles in the contiguous U.S.

5 WEST-CENTRAL

This heavily developed region is noted for its coastal marshes and mangrove forests, rivers, springs and extensive pine forests. The woodlands are interspersed with numerous hammocks that provide refuge for abundant deer, squirrels, hawks, owls and songbirds. The warm springs are the winter home of large numbers of manatees.

6 SOUTHWEST

The southwest is known for its serene, natural beauty. The northern part of this region is dominated by pine woodlands and the south is wetter, with many areas inundated with shallow water. The coastal barrier islands and mangrove-lined estuaries and bays harbor a rich array of plants and animals.

7 SOUTHEAST

This region encompasses unique areas including the coral forests of the Florida Keys and the grassy sea of the Everglades. The lush, tropical habitat supports the state's greatest diversity of plants and animals including dozens of threatened and endangered species.

NORTHWEST

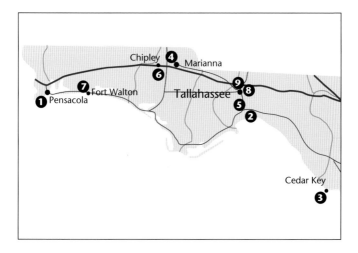

Parks/Wildlife Areas

❶ GULF ISLANDS NATIONAL SEASHORE
The pristine beaches and marshes of this 150 mile-long (240 km) sanctuary are a haven for wildlife including resident bottle-nosed dolphins, pelicans, raccoons, terns, and opossums. Facilities include a boat dock and ramp, visitor center and bookstore.
Website: www.nps.gov/guis

❷ SAINT MARKS NATIONAL WILDLIFE REFUGE
Marshes, hardwood swamps and pine-oak forests are prime birding territory. Visitor center highlights the local flora and fauna and extensive trail system.
Website: www.fws.gov/refuge/st_marks

❸ CEDAR KEYS NATIONAL WILDLIFE REFUGE
Expansive salt marsh and offshore islands are the nesting area of over 200,000 birds including egrets, pelicans and osprey.
Website: www.fws.gov/cedarkeys

❹ FLORIDA CAVERNS STATE PARK
Dry caverns feature impressive formations of stalactites, stalagmites and rock 'waterfalls'. Visitor center offers canoe rentals and ranger-guided tours.
Website: www.floridastateparks.org/park/Florida-Caverns

❺ EDWARD BALL WAKULLA SPRINGS STATE PARK
Home to the world's deepest and largest freshwater spring and the source of the Wakulla River. Nature trails and glass-bottom boat tours highlight the area's natural beauty. Anhingas, eagles, gallinules and herons are a few species found in this popular birding 'mecca'.
Website: www.floridastateparks.org/park/Wakulla-Springs

❻ FALLING WATERS STATE RECREATION AREA
Highlight is a 'sink' waterfall which plunges from ground level into a pit 100 ft. (30 m) deep. A popular hiking and camping destination, it features nature trails and an observation deck.
Website: www.floridastateparks.org/park/Falling-Waters

Museums/Attractions

❼ GULFARIUM
Exhibits highlight native aquatic mammals, reptiles and fresh and salt water fishes. Guided tours and a gift shop are available.
Website: www.gulfarium.com

❽ TALLAHASSEE MUSEUM OF HISTORY AND NATURAL SCIENCE
Exhibits highlight Florida's human and natural history. 100 native animals including panthers and alligators live in the surrounding woodland and cypress swamp habitat.
Website: www.tallahasseemuseum.org

❾ ALFRED B. MACLAY GARDENS STATE PARK
Rare native plants and exotics are highlighted on the grounds of this southern estate.
Website: www.floridastateparks.org/park/Maclay-Gardens

NORTHEAST

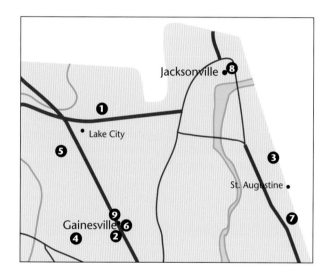

Parks/Wildlife Areas

① OSCEOLA NATIONAL FOREST
183,000 acre forest encompasses habitats including pine woodlands, cypress and bay swamps.
A popular hiking, fishing and camping destination, the area features dozens of rivers, creeks and sinkhole lakes.
Website: www.fs.usda.gov/osceola

② PAYNES PRAIRIE PRESERVE STATE PARK
21,000 acre wildlife sanctuary harbors an array of wildlife including otters, alligators, bison and resident sandhill cranes. Hiking, biking and horse trails wind through prairie, pine flatwoods and oak hammocks. Visitor center and museum.
Website: www.floridastateparks.org/park/Paynes-Prairie

③ GUANA RIVER WILDLIFE MANAGEMENT AREA
A few of the diverse wildlife species that inhabit or visit this minimally disturbed area include alligators, tortoises, deer, spoonbills, wood storks, herons, stilts, falcons, pelicans, hawks, kites and bald eagles.
Website: www.myfwc.com/viewing/recreation/wmas/lead/Guana-River

④ SAN FELASCO HAMMOCK PRESERVE STATE PARK
Outstanding woodland area encompasses forests of pine, maple and magnolia in addition to numerous sinkholes and ponds. An excellent birding destination, it has miles of maintained trails.
Website: www.floridastateparks.org/park/San-Felasco-Hammock

⑤ ICHETUCKNEE SPRINGS STATE PARK
The main attraction of this popular park is a slow-moving spring-fed river that is easy to float in a canoe or tube while admiring the scenery. Self-guided trails wind through the adjacent uplands.
Website: www.floridastateparks.org/park/Ichetucknee-Springs

Museums/Attractions

⑥ FLORIDA MUSEUM OF NATURAL HISTORY
Ranked among the top ten natural history museums in the country, it features dozens of ecological exhibits highlighting native plant and animal life.
Website: www.flmnh.ufl.edu

⑦ MARINELAND
Oceanfront attraction features exhibits on native marine life, reptiles and seashells from around the world.
Website: www.marineland.net

⑧ JACKSONVILLE ZOO & GARDENS
Features more than 800 species of mammals, birds and reptiles from around the world.
Website: www.jacksonvillezoo.org

⑨ KANAPAHA BOTANICAL GARDENS
The state's second largest and most diverse botanical garden features wildflower, medicinal herb, palm, hummingbird, rock, sunken, and carnivorous plant gardens.
Website: www.kanapaha.org

EAST-CENTRAL

Parks/Wildlife Areas

❶ CANAVERAL NATIONAL SEASHORE
Refuge protects the longest undeveloped tract of land on Florida's east coast. Noted for its miles of pristine beaches, tall sand dunes and mangrove islands. Manatees, alligators, sea turtles and over 275 bird species are a few of the area's natural attractions. Programs including ranger-guided walks and turtle watches are offered seasonally.
Website: www.nps.gov/cana

❷ TURKEY CREEK SANCTUARY
Popular sanctuary features a board-walk that passes through habitats ranging from sand pine scrub and hardwood hammocks to wet forests. Margaret Hames Nature Center provides information on local natural history.
Website: www.palmbayflorida.org/government/departments/parks-and-recreation/recreation/turkey-creek-sanctuary

❸ HOBE SOUND NATIONAL WILDLIFE REFUGE
Area's beaches are one of the most important nesting areas for sea turtles in the U.S. Resident birds include osprey, pelicans and jays. Guided walks and interpretive programs are offered seasonally by the Hobe Sound Nature Center.
Website: www.fws.gov/refuge/hobe_sound/

❹ MERRITT ISLAND NATIONAL WILDLIFE REFUGE
One of the state's most popular wildlife viewing destinations, it is home to over 290 species of birds including egrets, ibis, spoonbills, bald eagles, peregrine falcons, pelicans, storks and scrub jays. If you time your visit right, you may also observe endangered sea turtles and manatees. A number of roads and trails offer excellent access throughout the sanctuary. Visitor center features interpretive displays. A photo blind and observation tower are also located on site.
Website: www.fws.gov/refuge/Merritt_Island

❺ LAKE WOODRUFF NATIONAL WILDLIFE REFUGE
The main attraction of this 19,000 acre sanctuary is miles of diked wetlands that provide prime habitat for waterfowl and marsh birds. Resident alligators and otters can also be spotted and manatees move into the refuge between May and June.
Website: www.fws.gov/lakewoodruff

Museums/Attractions

❻ MUSEUM OF ARTS & SCIENCES
One wing of the complex high-lights the natural history of Florida and features a rare skeleton of a 130,000 year-old giant sloth.
Website: www.moas.org

❼ SEA WORLD
The world's largest marine zoological park features exhibits and shows "designed to promote a better understanding of the marine world and show how it is threatened by human thoughtlessness".
Website: www.seaworldparks.com

CENTRAL

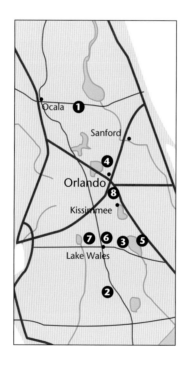

Parks/Wildlife Areas

❶ OCALA NATIONAL FOREST
Unique area supports the world's largest scrub community and is often called the 'Big Scrub.' Here you'll find vast sand pine forests growing on dunes over 100 ft. (31 m) deep in places. The forest is nearly surrounded by the St. Johns and Oklawaha rivers, and a popular activity is to explore the lush, semi-tropical forests by canoe. Over two dozen species of plants and animals are endemic to this area.
Website: www.fs.usda.gov/ocala

❷ HIGHLANDS HAMMOCK STATE PARK
One of Florida's first state parks, the area protects a number of plant communities including a rare virgin hardwood forest and cypress swamps. Visitors can explore the park on several easy nature trails or take guided tram tours to more remote areas.
Website: www.floridastateparks. org/park/Highlands-Hammock

❸ LAKE KISSIMMEE STATE PARK
The pine flatwoods, dense scrub and floodplain prairies surrounding Florida's third largest lake support dozens of rare animals including sandhill cranes, scrub jays, snail kites and burrowing owls. Deer, turkeys, bobwhites and songbirds are abundant.
Website: www.floridastateparks. org/park/Lake-Kissimmee

❹ WEKIWA SPRINGS STATE PARK
The park's diverse plant communities – ranging from palm-oak hammocks to pine sandhills – support bears, otters, eagles, ospreys, foxes, opossums and bobcats to name a few. Hiking, horseback riding and river floating are three ways to experience the beauty of this popular recreation area.
Website: www.floridastateparks. org/park/Wekiwa-Springs

❺ THREE LAKES WILDLIFE MANAGEMENT AREA
The Prairie Lakes area within this preserve is home to the highest concentration of nesting bald eagles in the contiguous U.S. Bobwhites, sandhill cranes, hawks, deer, turkeys and wild hogs are also abundant.
Website: http://myfwc.com/ viewing/recreation/wmas/lead/ three-lakes

Museums/Attractions

❻ BOK TOWER GARDENS
Thousands of native and exotic plants are featured in this botanical sanctuary. Facilities include a nature observatory and visitor center.
Website: www.boktower gardens.org

❼ CYPRESS GARDENS
Themed gardens feature over 8,000 varieties of plants from around the world. Butterfly conservatory is also located on site.
Website: www.florida.legoland. com/en/EXPLORE-THE-PARK/Park-Map/Cypress-Gardens

❽ DISCOVERY COVE
Adventure park features underwater walking tours and interactive nature experiences with dolphins, otters and birds. Ranked #1 amusement park in the world in 2014 by Tripadvisor.
Website: www.discoverycove.com

WEST-CENTRAL

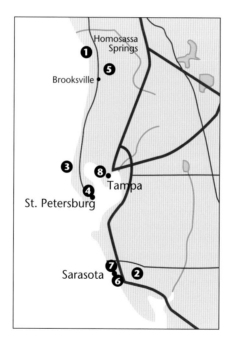

Parks/Wildlife Areas

❶ HOMOSASSA SPRINGS STATE WILDLIFE STATE PARK
Warm spring waters in this park attract abundant marine life. An excellent underwater viewing area allows visitors to observe hundreds of fish and manatees in their natural environment. Native birds, reptiles and mammals can be viewed in outdoor enclosures. Guided boat tours and a children's education center are also available.
Website: www.floridastateparks. org/park/Homosassa-Springs

❷ MYAKKA RIVER STATE PARK
Park features a combination of marshes, hammocks, prairies, rivers and lakes that support wildlife including alligators, deer, raccoons and more than 200 bird species. Best wildlife viewing is along the scenic river in a rented canoe. Interpretive center offers nature tours on a seasonal basis.
Website: www.floridastateparks. org/park/Myakka-River

❸ HONEYMOON ISLAND STATE PARK
Nature lovers will find osprey nests, a wide variety of shorebirds, and one of the few remaining virgin slash pine forests in South Florida. The park boasts several nature trails and bird observation areas.
Website: www.florida stateparks.org/park/Honeymoon-Island

❹ BOYD HILL NATURE PARK
Miles of trails meander through habitats including sand pine scrub, hardwood hammock, pine flatwoods and marshes. An excellent birding destination in the heart of a bustling city.
Website: www.stpeteparksrec. org/boyd-hill-nature-preserve.html

❺ WITHLACOOCHEE STATE FOREST
Forest has six separate tracts that encompass over 113,000 acres of cypress, pine and oak forests, prairies and hammocks. Forestry center provides maps and brochures and is located north of Brooksville on U.S. Route 41.
Website: www.floridaforest service.com

Museums/Attractions

❻ MOTE MARINE AQUARIUM
Displays feature plants and animals native to the Gulf of Mexico. Attractions include a large touch tank and a 135,000 gallon outdoor shark tank.
Website: www.mote.org

❼ MARIE SELBY BOTANICAL GARDENS
Lush gardens highlight native and exotic species including air plants, orchids, bromeliads, pitcher plants, palms and mangroves. Also features butterfly garden and museum.
Website: www.selby.org

❽ THE FLORIDA AQUARIUM
Over 4,300 aquatic plants and animals are featured in this state-of-the-art facility. Interactive displays highlight Florida's ecosystems. Dolphin cruises take visitors out see wild species in Tampa Bay.
Website: www.flaquarium.org

SOUTHWEST

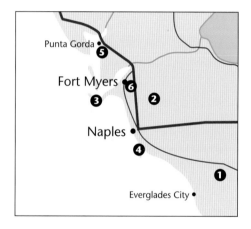

Parks/Wildlife Areas

❶ BIG CYPRESS NATIONAL PRESERVE

Referred to by many as a swamp, the preserve encompasses prairies, mixed hardwood hammocks, sandy islands of slash pine, mangrove forests and waterways bordered by thick belts of dwarf cypress trees. Area is named for the rare old-growth bald cypress trees still found here. The preserve is flooded for much of the year and its nutrient-rich waters support a rich aquatic fauna. Visitor center has numerous displays on local plant and animal life.
Website: www.nps.gov/bicy

❷ CORKSCREW SWAMP SANCTUARY

Refuge encompasses a wide range of habitats including pinelands, marshes, wet prairie and the world's largest ancient bald cypress forest. Two mile long boardwalk winds through the sanctuary. Area is the nesting home of rare birds including wood storks and swallow-tailed kites. Visitor center.
Website: corkscrew.audubon.org

❸ J.N. 'DING' DARLING NATIONAL WILDLIFE REFUGE

One of the most popular refuges in Florida, it encompasses 5,000 acres of wetlands and island uplands that are home to over 280 species of birds, 50 reptiles and amphibians and 30 mammals. Refuge features a number of interpretive and marked canoe trails, an observation tower and marinas. Many experts consider Sanibel Island to be the best shell-collecting area in the western hemisphere. Excellent visitor center.
Website: www.dingdarling society.org

Museums/Attractions

❹ THE CONSERVANCY BRIGGS NATURE CENTER

Interpretive center offers naturalist-led tours of the marshes, mangrove forests and pine flatwoods of the Rookery Bay National Estuarine Research Reserve. Visitors can explore the area by pontoon boat, canoe or nature trail. Wildlife is abundant and easily observed.
Website: www.conservancy.org/nature-center/briggs-boardwalk-wildlife

❺ CHARLOTTE HARBOR ENVIRONMENTAL CENTER

Located on a 3,000 acre sanctuary, the center features exhibits of the area's ecosystems, a touch tank and a museum annex. The environmental center is split into two facilities which include the alligator creek preserve and the cedar point park. Alligators, turtles and a variety of marsh and songbirds can be observed from trails winding through the refuge.
Website: checflorida.org

❻ CALUSA NATURE CENTER & PLANETARIUM

Exhibits highlight Florida's native plants, animals and habitats. Planetarium features star and laser shows and large screen films.
Website: www.calusanature.org

SOUTHEAST

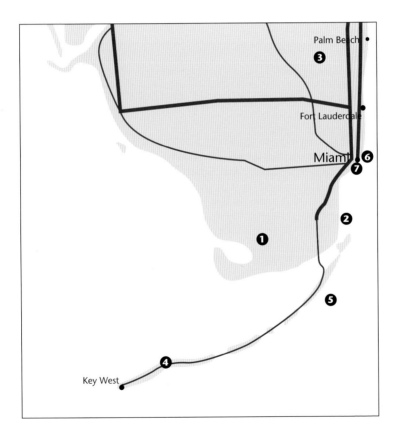

Parks/Wildlife Areas

❶ EVERGLADES NATIONAL PARK
This 1.4 million-acre sub-tropical wilderness encompasses a patch-work of ecosystems including mangrove forests, estuaries, freshwater sloughs, sawgrass prairies, tree islands (hardwood hammocks) and pine uplands. Much of the park is submerged beneath a shallow slow-moving stream that drains southern Florida. The nutrient-rich waters support an incredible diversity of life including over 300 species of birds and 600 species of fishes, reptiles and amphibians. Key attractions include Ten Thousand Islands, Shark Valley and Mahogany Hammock. The area features a number of interpretive trails, and boats and bikes can be rented at several locations.
Website: www.nps.gov/ever

❷ BISCAYNE NATIONAL PARK
Sub-tropical wilderness and recreation area features miles of living coral reefs, mangrove forests and a number of small islands. Ninety-five percent of the park is underwater, and the clear water and abundant marine life attract divers from around the world.
Website: www.nps.gov/bisc

❸ ARTHUR R. MARSHALL LOXAHATCHEE NATIONAL WILDLIFE REFUGE
Wetland wilderness area supports a diverse array of bird life including thousands of nesting egrets, herons and ibises and 13 threatened or endangered species. Several hiking and canoe trails allow visitors to penetrate the heart of this pristine wilderness. Visitor center.
Website: www.fws.gov/ loxahatchee

❹ NATIONAL KEY DEER REFUGE
Tropical refuge protects the last remaining population of key deer, a diminutive subspecies of whitetail. Area features viewing platforms and interpretive trails.
Website: www.fws.gov/ nationalkeydeer

❺ JOHN PENNEKAMP CORAL REEF STATE PARK
Park protects a portion of the only living coral reef in the continental U.S. Area is renowned for its spec-tacular marine life. Concessions offer glass-bottom boat tours, diving and snorkeling adventures.
Website: www.pennekamp park.com

Museums/Attractions

❻ MIAMI SEAQUARIUM
60-acre facility features a variety of exhibits and interactive displays that promote a greater understanding of native fish, marine mammals and birds.
Website: www.miami seaquarium.com

❼ MIAMI MUSEUM OF SCIENCE & PLANETARIUM
Features dozens of displays and exhibits on native plants and animals. Wildlife Center exhibits a number of live birds, reptiles and other native animals.
Website: www.miamisci.org

MAMMALS

- ❏ Black Bear
- ❏ Black Rat
- ❏ Bobcat
- ❏ Bottlenose Dolphin
- ❏ Brazilian Free-tailed Bat
- ❏ Common Dolphin
- ❏ Common Gray Fox
- ❏ Common Raccoon
- ❏ Common Red Fox
- ❏ Cotton Mouse
- ❏ Coyote
- ❏ Eastern Cottontail
- ❏ Eastern Gray Squirrel
- ❏ Eastern Mole
- ❏ Eastern Spotted Skunk
- ❏ Florida Panther
- ❏ Florida Water Rat
- ❏ Florida Woodrat
- ❏ Fox Squirrel
- ❏ Hispid Cotton Rat
- ❏ House Mouse
- ❏ Humpback Whale
- ❏ Least Shrew
- ❏ Manatee
- ❏ Marsh Rabbit
- ❏ Mink
- ❏ Nine-banded Armadillo
- ❏ Northern River Otter
- ❏ Norway Rat
- ❏ Nutria
- ❏ Short-finned Pilot Whale
- ❏ Southeastern Bat
- ❏ Southeastern Pocket Gopher
- ❏ Southern Flying Squirrel
- ❏ Striped Skunk
- ❏ Virginia Opossum
- ❏ White-tailed Deer
- ❏ Wild Boar

BIRDS

- ❏ American Avocet
- ❏ American Black Duck
- ❏ American Coot
- ❏ American Crow
- ❏ American Flamingo
- ❏ American Goldfinch
- ❏ American Kestrel
- ❏ American Oystercatcher
- ❏ American Robin
- ❏ American White Pelican
- ❏ Anhinga
- ❏ Bald Eagle
- ❏ Baltimore Oriole
- ❏ Belted Kingfisher
- ❏ Black-bellied Plover
- ❏ Black-crowned Night-Heron
- ❏ Black-necked Stilt
- ❏ Black Skimmer
- ❏ Black Vulture
- ❏ Blue Jay
- ❏ Blue-winged Teal
- ❏ Boat-tailed Grackle
- ❏ Brown Pelican
- ❏ Brown Thrasher
- ❏ Burrowing Owl
- ❏ Carolina Chickadee
- ❏ Carolina Wren
- ❏ Cedar Waxwing
- ❏ Chipping Sparrow
- ❏ Common Grackle
- ❏ Common Nighthawk
- ❏ Common Yellowthroat
- ❏ Crested Caracara
- ❏ Double-crested Cormorant
- ❏ Downy Woodpecker
- ❏ Eastern Bluebird
- ❏ Eastern Kingbird
- ❏ Eastern Meadowlark
- ❏ Eastern Phoebe
- ❏ Eastern Screech Owl
- ❏ Eastern Towhee
- ❏ Eurasian Collared Dove
- ❏ European Starling
- ❏ Fish Crow
- ❏ Florida Scrub-Jay
- ❏ Glossy Ibis
- ❏ Great Blue Heron
- ❏ Great Crested Flycatcher
- ❏ Great Egret
- ❏ Great Horned Owl
- ❏ Greater Yellowlegs
- ❏ Green Heron
- ❏ Green-winged Teal
- ❏ Hairy Woodpecker
- ❏ Herring Gull
- ❏ House Sparrow
- ❏ Indigo Bunting
- ❏ Killdeer
- ❏ Laughing Gull
- ❏ Lesser Yellowlegs
- ❏ Limpkin
- ❏ Magnificent Frigatebird
- ❏ Mallard
- ❏ Mottled Duck
- ❏ Mourning Dove
- ❏ Northern Bobwhite
- ❏ Northern Cardinal

❏ Northern Flicker
❏ Northern Mockingbird
❏ Northern Shoveler
❏ Orchard Oriole
❏ Osprey
❏ Painted Bunting
❏ Palm Warbler
❏ Pied-billed Grebe
❏ Pileated Woodpecker
❏ Pine Warbler
❏ Purple Martin
❏ Red-bellied Woodpecker
❏ Red-breasted Merganser
❏ Red-headed Woodpecker
❏ Red-shouldered Hawk
❏ Red-tailed Hawk
❏ Red-winged Blackbird
❏ Ring-billed Gull
❏ Ring-necked Duck
❏ Rock Pigeon
❏ Roseate Spoonbill
❏ Royal Tern
❏ Ruby-throated Hummingbird
❏ Ruddy Duck
❏ Ruddy Turnstone
❏ Sanderling
❏ Sandhill Crane
❏ Snowy Egret
❏ Swallow-tailed Kite
❏ Tree Swallow
❏ Tufted Titmouse
❏ Turkey Vulture
❏ White Ibis
❏ Wild Turkey
❏ Willet
❏ Wood Duck
❏ Wood Stork
❏ Yellow-billed Cattle Egret
❏ Yellow-billed Cuckoo
❏ Yellow-rumped Warbler

REPTILES & AMPHIBIANS

❏ Alligator Snapping Turtle
❏ American Alligator
❏ American Crocodile
❏ Bullfrog
❏ Burmese Python
❏ Cuban Brown Anole
❏ Dusky Pigmy Rattlesnake
❏ Eastern Coral Snake
❏ Eastern Corn Snake
❏ Eastern Diamondback
  Rattlesnake
❏ Eastern Fence Lizard

❏ Eastern Garter Snake
❏ Eastern Hognose Snake
❏ Florida Cottonmouth
❏ Florida Redbelly Cooter
❏ Florida Snapping Turtle
❏ Florida Softshell
❏ Gopher Tortoise
❏ Green Anole
❏ Green Sea Turtle
❏ Green Treefrog
❏ Leatherback Sea Turtle
❏ Loggerhead Sea Turtle
❏ Mediterranean Gecko
❏ Oak Toad
❏ Peninsular Cooter
❏ Pig Frog
❏ Red-eared Slider
❏ Scarlet Kingsnake
❏ Slimy Salamander
❏ Southeastern Five-lined Skink
❏ Southern Black Racer
❏ Southern Cricket Frog
❏ Southern Leopard Frog
❏ Southern Ringneck Snake
❏ Southern Toad
❏ Spectacled Caiman

FISHES

❏ American Eel
❏ Atlantic Menhaden
❏ Atlantic Spadefish
❏ Black Crappie
❏ Black Drum
❏ Blue Marlin
❏ Blue Tang
❏ Bluegill
❏ Bluehead
❏ Bonefish
❏ Bowfin
❏ Brook Silversides
❏ Brown Bullhead
❏ Chain Pickerel
❏ Channel Catfish
❏ Cobia
❏ Common Carp
❏ Dolphinfish
❏ Florida Pompano
❏ Gafftopsail Catfish
❏ Gar
❏ Golden Shiner
❏ Grass Carp
❏ Great Barracuda
❏ Green Moray
❏ Gulf Flounder

SPECIES CHECKLIST

- ❏ Gulf Pipefish
- ❏ Largemouth Bass
- ❏ Longspine Squirrelfish
- ❏ Lookdown
- ❏ Mosquitofish
- ❏ Nurse Shark
- ❏ Pinfish
- ❏ Queen Angelfish
- ❏ Queen Parrotfish
- ❏ Queen Triggerfish
- ❏ Redear Sunfish
- ❏ Redfin Pickerel
- ❏ Red Grouper
- ❏ Redbreast Sunfish
- ❏ Sailfin Molly
- ❏ Sailfish
- ❏ Schoolmaster
- ❏ Sea Lamprey
- ❏ Sergeant Major
- ❏ Sheepshead
- ❏ Snook
- ❏ Spotfin Butterflyfish
- ❏ Striped Anchovy
- ❏ Striped Bass
- ❏ Striped Mullet
- ❏ Swamp Darter
- ❏ Tarpon
- ❏ White Cappie
- ❏ White Grunt

SEASHORE LIFE

- ❏ Acorn Barnacle
- ❏ Alternate Tellin
- ❏ Angel Wing
- ❏ Atlantic Bay Scallop
- ❏ Atlantic Purple Sea Urchin
- ❏ Atlantic Slipper Snail
- ❏ Beach Flea
- ❏ Blue Crab
- ❏ Calico Scallop
- ❏ Common Baby's Ear
- ❏ Common Eastern Dog Whelk
- ❏ Common Jingle Shell
- ❏ Common Purple Sea Snail
- ❏ Common Sea Star
- ❏ Cushion Star
- ❏ Eastern Oyster
- ❏ Eelgrass
- ❏ Fiddler Crab
- ❏ Florida Coquina
- ❏ Florida Horse Conch
- ❏ Florida Lace Murex
- ❏ Ghost Crab
- ❏ Giant Atlantic Cockle

- ❏ Glasswort
- ❏ Gooseneck Barnacle
- ❏ Great Land Crab
- ❏ Hermit Crab
- ❏ Hooked Mussel
- ❏ Horseshoe Crab
- ❏ Keyhole Urchin
- ❏ Labyrinthine Brain Coral
- ❏ Lettered Olive
- ❏ Lightning Whelk
- ❏ Long-spined Sea Urchin
- ❏ Moon Jellyfish
- ❏ Pink Shrimp
- ❏ Portuguese Man-of-War
- ❏ Queen Helmet
- ❏ Sail Jellyfish
- ❏ Salt Marsh Cordgrass
- ❏ Sargassum Weed
- ❏ Saw-toothed Pen Shell
- ❏ Scotch Bonnet
- ❏ Sea Lettuce
- ❏ Sea Oats
- ❏ Staghorn Coral
- ❏ Sunray Venus Clam
- ❏ Thick-lipped Oyster Drill
- ❏ Turtle Grass
- ❏ Wentletrap

TREES & SHRUBS

- ❏ American Beech
- ❏ American Holly
- ❏ Australian Pine
- ❏ Baldcypress
- ❏ Brazilian Pepper
- ❏ Cabbage Palm
- ❏ Chinese Tallow
- ❏ Coconut Palm
- ❏ Common Persimmon
- ❏ Dahoon
- ❏ Dove Plum
- ❏ Florida Royal Palm
- ❏ Florida Strangler Fig
- ❏ Gumbo-Limbo
- ❏ Laurel Oak
- ❏ Live Oak
- ❏ Longleaf Pine
- ❏ Manila Plum
- ❏ Marlberry
- ❏ Mockernut Hickory
- ❏ Punk Tree
- ❏ Red Bay
- ❏ Red Mangrove
- ❏ Red Maple
- ❏ Sand Pine

❏ Saw Palmetto
❏ Seagrape
❏ Shortleaf Fig
❏ Slash Pine
❏ Southeastern Coralbean
❏ Southern Magnolia
❏ Southern Red Cedar
❏ Southern Red Oak
❏ Southern Waxmyrtle
❏ Sweetbay
❏ Sweetgum
❏ Tuliptree (Yellow Poplar)
❏ Turkey Oak
❏ Washingtonia
❏ Water Oak
❏ Yaupon

WILDFLOWERS
White
❏ Aloe Yucca
❏ Arrowhead
❏ Atamasco Lily
❏ Beggartick
❏ Buttonbush
❏ Fragrant Water Lily
❏ Gopher Apple
❏ Indian Pipe
❏ Jimsonweed
❏ Lamb's Quarters
❏ Lizard's Tail
❏ Moonflower
❏ Musky Mint
❏ Queen Anne's Lace
❏ Red Clover
❏ String Lily
❏ Sneezeweed
❏ Swamp Rose Mallow
❏ Tread Softly
❏ White Clover
❏ White Sweet Clover

Yellow, Orange & Green
❏ Atlantic St. John's Wort
❏ Black-eyed Susan
❏ Butterflyweed
❏ Century Plant
❏ Common Cattail
❏ Common Evening Primrose
❏ Common Mullein
❏ Common Plantain
❏ Common Sunflower
❏ Florida Butterfly Orchid
❏ Giant Air Plant
❏ Hooded Pitcher Plant

❏ Lotus Lily
❏ Partridge Pea
❏ Prickly Pear Cactus
❏ Sacred Lotus
❏ Spanish Daisy
❏ Spanish Moss
❏ Stick-tight
❏ Tickseed
❏ Wild Senna
❏ Yellow Bachelor's Button
❏ Yellow Buttons
❏ Yellow Jessamine
❏ Yellow Pond Lily

Red & Pink
❏ Blazing Star
❏ Butterfly Pea
❏ Cardinal Flower
❏ Chicory
❏ Christmas Poinsettia
❏ Common Fleabane
❏ Fern Rose
❏ Firewheel
❏ Grass Pink Orchid
❏ Lady's Thumb
❏ Lantana
❏ Meadow Beauty
❏ Pine Lily
❏ Pink Purslane
❏ Pink Sundew
❏ Red Clover
❏ Rose Mallow
❏ Skyrocket
❏ Swamp Milkweed
❏ Tropical Sage
❏ Trumpet Honeysuckle
❏ Wild Poinsettia

Blue & Purple
❏ Aster
❏ Blue Toadflax
❏ Blue-eyed Grass
❏ Carolina Wild Petunia
❏ Chicory
❏ Dayflower
❏ Hollow Joe-Pye-Weed
❏ Iris
❏ Mistflower
❏ Passionflower
❏ Pickerelweed
❏ Sea Lavender
❏ Vervain
❏ Water Hyacinth

GLOSSARY

Alternate
Spaced singly along the stem.

Anther
The part of the stamen that produces pollen.

Anadromous
Living in saltwater, breeding in freshwater.

Annual
A plant which completes its life cycle in one year.

Anterior
Pertaining to the front end.

Aquatic
Living in water.

Aquifer
Underground chamber or layer of rock that holds water.

Ascending
Rising or curving upward.

Barbel
An organ near the mouth of fish used to taste, touch, or smell.

Barrier Island
Sandbar off the mainland that protects the coast from wave action.

Berry
A fruit formed from a single ovary which is fleshy or pulpy and contains one or many seeds.

Bloom
A whitish powdery or waxy covering.

Boss
A rounded knob between the eyes of some toads.

Brackish
Water that is part fresh water and part salt water.

Bract
A modified – often scale-like – leaf, usually small.

Branchlet
A twig from which leaves grow.

Burrow
A tunnel excavated and inhabited by an animal.

Carnivorous
Feeding primarily on meat.

Catkin
A caterpillar-like drooping cluster of small flowers.

Cold-blooded
Refers to animals that are unable to regulate their own body temperature. 'Ectotherm' is the preferred term for this characteristic since many 'cold-blooded' species like reptiles are at times able to maintain a warmer body temperature than that of 'warm-blooded' species like mammals.

Conifer
A cone-bearing tree, usually evergreen.

Coral
The limestone skeletal deposits of coral polyps.

Coverts
Small feathers that cover the underside (undertail) or top (uppertail) of the base of bird's tail.

Deciduous
Shedding leaves annually.

Dicots
Plants with two embryonic leaves at germination, net-veined leaves, stems with cylindrical vascular bundles in a regular pattern that contain cambium.

Diurnal
Active primarily during the day.

Dorsal
Pertaining to the back or upper surface.

Ecology
The study of the relationships between organisms, and between organisms and their environment.

Endangered
Species threatened with extinction.

Epiphyte
A plant that obtains nourishment from nutrients in the air and rain. They often live on host plants like trees without harming them.

Endemic
Living only in a particular area.

Estuary
A partially enclosed body of water where inland freshwater mixes with sea water.

Flower
Reproductive structure of a plant.

Flower stalk
The stem bearing the flowers.

Fruit
The matured, seed-bearing ovary.

Gamete
An egg or sperm cell.

Habitat
The physical area in which organisms live.

Herbivorous
Feeding primarily on vegetation.

Insectivorous
Feeding primarily on insects.

Introduced
Species brought by humans to an area outside its normal range.

Invertebrate
Animals lacking backbones, e.g., worms, slugs, crustaceans, insects, shellfish.

Larva
Immature forms of an animal which differ from the adult.

Lateral
Located away from the mid-line, at or near the sides.

Lobe
A projecting part of a leaf or flower, usually rounded.

Molting
Loss of feathers, hair or skin while renewing plumage, coat or scales.

Monocots
Plants with one embryonic leaf at germination, parallel-veined leaves, stems with scattered vascular bundles with little or no cambium.

Morphs
A color variation of a species that is regular and not related to sex, age or season.

Nest
A structure built for shelter or insulation.

Nocturnal
Active primarily at night.

Omnivorous
Feeding on both animal and vegetable matter.

Ovary
The female sex organ which is the site of egg production and maturation.

Perennial
A plant that lives for several years.

Petal
The colored outer parts of a flower head.

Phase
Coloration other than typical.

Pistil
The central organ of the flower which develops into a fruit.

Pollen
The tiny grains produced in the anthers which contain the male reproductive cells.

Posterior
Pertaining to the rear.

Sepal
The outer, usually green, leaf-like structures that protect the flower bud and are located at the base of an open flower.

Species
A group of interbreeding organisms which are reproductively isolated from other groups.

Speculum
A brightly colored, iridescent patch on the wings of some birds, especially ducks.

Spur
A pointed projection.

Subspecies
A relatively uniform, distinct portion of a species population.

Threatened
Species not yet endangered but in imminent danger of being so.

Ungulate
A hoofed mammal.

Ventral
Pertaining to the under or lower surface.

Vertebrate
An animal possessing a backbone.

Warm-blooded
An animal which regulates its blood temperature internally. 'Endotherm' is the preferred term for this characteristic.

Whorl
A circle of leaves or flowers about a stem.

Woolly
Bearing long or matted hairs.

BIBLIOGRAPHY

MAMMALS
Boitani, Luigi and Stefania Bartoli. *Simon & Schuster's Guide to Mammals.* New York: Simon & Schuster, 1983.
Brown, Larry N. *Florida Mammals.* Miami: Windward Publishing, 1996.
Burt, William Henry. *A Field Guide to the Mammals: Field Marks of All North American Species Found North of Mexico.* 3rd ed. Boston: Houghton Mifflin, 1976.
Carwardine, Mark. *Eyewitness Handbooks: Whales, Dolphins and Porpoises.* New York: Dorling Kindersley, 1995.
Gingerich, Jerry Lee. *Florida's Fabulous Mammals.* Tampa: World Publications, 1994.
Murie, Olaus J. *A Field Guide to Animal Tracks.* 2nd ed. Boston: Houghton Mifflin, 1982.
Walker, Ernest P., et al. *Mammals of the World.* 2 vols. Baltimore: Johns Hopkins Press, 1965.
Whitaker, John O., Jr. *National Audubon Society Field Guide to North American Mammals.* Rev. ed. New York: Alfred A. Knopf, 1996.
Wilson, Don E. and Sue Ruff, eds. *The Smithsonian Book of North American Mammals.* Washington, D.C.: Smithsonian Institution Press, 1999.

BIRDS
Alsop, Fred J. III. *Smithsonian Handbooks Birds of North America: Eastern Region.* New York: Dorling Kindersley, 2001.
Barnard, Edward S. and Sharon Fass Yates, eds. *Reader's Digest North American Wildlife: Birds.* Pleasantville: Reader's Digest Association, 1998.
Bull, John and John Farrand, Jr. *The Audubon Society Field Guide to North American Birds: Eastern Region.* New York: Alfred A. Knopf, 1992.
Hall, Francis Wyly. *Birds of Florida.* 2nd Rev. ed. St. Petersburg: Great Outdoors Publishing, 1994.
Kale, Herbert W. and David S. Maehr. *Florida's Birds: A Handbook and Reference.* Sarasota: Pineapple Press, 1990.
Latimer, Jonathan P., et al. *Birds of North America: A Guide to Field Identification.* Rev. and updated. New York: St. Martin's Press, 2001.
National Geographic Field Guide to the Birds of North America. 4th ed. Washington, D.C.: National Geographic Society, 1987.
Peterson, Roger Tory. *A Field Guide to Eastern Birds.* 4th ed. Boston: Houghton Mifflin, 1980.
Robbins, C.S., et al. *Birds of North America.* New York: Golden Press, 1988.
Sibley, David Allen. *The Sibley Guide to Birds.* New York: Alfred A. Knopf, 2000.
Williams, Winston. *Florida's Fabulous Birds.* Tampa: World Wide Printing, 1986.

REPTILES & AMPHIBIANS
Ashton R.E., Jr., and P.S. Ashton. *Handbook of Reptiles and Amphibians of Florida.* Parts 1-3. Miami: Windward Publishing, 1991.
Behler, John L. *National Audubon Society Field Guide to North American Reptiles and Amphibians.* New York: Alfred A. Knopf, 1979.
Carmichael, Pete and Winston Williams. *Florida's Fabulous Reptiles and Amphibians.* Tampa: World Publications, 1991.
Conant, R. and J.T. Collins. *A Field Guide to Reptiles and Amphibians: Eastern and Central North America.* Boston: Houghton Mifflin, 1991.
Smith, Hobart M. and Edmund D. Brodie, Jr. *Reptiles of North America: A Guide to Field Identification.* New York: St. Martin's Press, 1982.
Stebbins, Robert C. *A Field Guide to Western Reptiles and Amphibians.* 2nd ed. Boston: Houghton Mifflin, 1985.
Zim, Herbert S. and Hobart M. Smith. *Reptiles and Amphibians.* Rev. ed. New York: Golden Press, 1987.

FISHES & SEASHORE LIFE
Abbott, R. Tucker. *Seashells of North America: A Guide to Field Identification.* New York: Golden Press, 1968.
Allyn, Rube. *Florida Fishes: Saltwater.* Rev. ed. St. Petersburg: Great Outdoors Publishing, 1982.
Boschung, H.T., et al. *The Audubon Society Field Guide to North American Fishes, Whales and Dolphins.* New York: Alfred A. Knopf, 1989.
Gilbert, Carter R. and James D. Williams. *National Audubon Society Field Guide to Fishes: North America.* Rev. ed. New York: Alfred A. Knopf, 2002.
Kaplan, Eugene H. *A Field Guide to Coral Reefs: Caribbean and Florida.* Boston: Houghton Mifflin, 1982.
Kaplan, Eugene H. *A Field Guide to Southeastern and Caribbean Seashores: Cape Hatteras to the Gulf Coast, Florida, and the Caribbean.* Boston: Houghton Mifflin, 1988.
Lieske, Ewald and Robert Myers. *Coral Reef Fishes: Indo-Pacific and Caribbean.* Rev. ed. Princeton: Princeton University Press, 2002.
Meinkoth, Norman A. *National Audubon Society Field Guide to North American Seashore Creatures.* New York: Alfred A. Knopf, 1998.
Miller, Arthur P., Jr., and Marjorie L. Miller. *Park Ranger Guide to Seashores.* Harrisburg: Stackpole Books, 1992.

Page, Lawrence and Brooks M. Burr. *A Field Guide to Freshwater Fishes: North America North of Mexico.* Boston: Houghton Mifflin, 1991.

Rehder, Harald A. *The Audubon Society Guide to North American Seashells.* New York: Alfred A. Knopf, 2000.

Robins, C. Richard, et al. *A Field Guide to Atlantic Coast Fishes: North America.* Boston: Houghton Mifflin, 1986.

Smith, C. Lavett. *National Audubon Society Field Guide to Tropical Marine Fishes of the Caribbean, the Gulf of Mexico, Florida, the Bahamas, and Bermuda.* New York: Alfred A. Knopf, 2002.

Waller, Geoffrey, ed. *SeaLife: A Complete Guide to the Marine Environment.* Washington, D.C.: Smithsonian Institution Press, 1996.

FLORA

Anderson, Robert. *Guide to Florida Wildflowers.* Coral Gables: Winner Enterprises, 1989.

Barnard, Edward S. and Sharon Fass Yates, eds. *Reader's Digest North American Wildlife: Wildflowers.* Pleasantville: Reader's Digest Association, 1998.

Bell, C.R. and B.J. Taylor. *The Trees of Florida.* Chapel Hill: Laurel Hill Press, 1992.

Clewell, Andre F. *Guide to the Vascular Plants of the Florida Panhandle.* Tallahassee: Florida State University Press, 1985.

Coombes, Allen J. *Eye Witness Handbooks: Trees.* New York: Dorling Kindersley, 1992.

Craighead, Frank C. *The Trees of Southern Florida.* Coral Gables: University of Miami Press, 1971.

Duncan, Wilbur H and Marion B. Duncan. *Trees of the Southeastern U.S.* Athens: University of Georgia Press, 1988.

Elias, Thomas S. *The Complete Trees of North America: Field Guide and Natural History.* New York: Van Nostrand Reinhold, 1980.

Kricher, John C. *A Field Guide to the Ecology of Eastern Forests: North America.* Boston: Houghton Mifflin, 1988.

Lanzara, Paoloa and Mariella Pizzetti. *Simon & Schuster's Guide to Trees.* New York: Simon & Schuster, 1978.

Little, Elbert L. *National Audubon Society Field Guide to North American Trees: Eastern Region.* New York: Alfred A. Knopf, 1980.

Long, Robert W., and Olga Lakela. *Flora of Tropical Florida.* Coral Gables: University of Miami Press, 1971.

Parker, Richard. *Wildflowers.* Miami: Windward Publishing, 1986.

Procter, Lucille. *Handbook of Florida Flowers.* St. Petersburg: Great Outdoors Publishing, 1959.

Stevenson, George B. *Trees of Everglades National Park and the Florida Keys.* 2nd ed. George B. Stevenson, 1969.

Thieret, John W. *National Audubon Society Field Guide to North American Wildflowers: Eastern Region.* Rev. ed. New York: Alfred A. Knopf, 2001.

Venning, Frank D. *Wildflowers of North America: A Guide to Field Identification.* New York: Golden Press, 1984.

Williams, Winston. *Florida's Fabulous Flowers.* Tampa: World Publications, 1986.

Wunderlin, Richard P. *Guide to the Vascular Plants of Central Florida.* Tampa: University of South Florida Press, 1982.

NATURAL HISTORY

Alden, Peter, et al. *National Audubon Society Field Guide to Florida.* New York: Alfred A. Knopf, 2000.

Benyus, Janine M. *The Field Guide to Wildlife Habitats of the Eastern United States.* New York: Simon & Schuster, 1989.

Cerulean, Susan and Ann Morrow. *Florida Wildlife Viewing Guide.* Helena: Falcon Press, 1998.

Grow, Gerald. *Florida Parks: A Guide to Camping in Nature.* Tallahassee: Longleaf Publications, 1989.

Jewell, Susan D. *Exploring Wild South Florida.* Sarasota: Pineapple Press, 1993.

Lantz, Peggy S. and Wendy Hale. *The Young Naturalist's Guide to Florida.* Sarasota: Pineapple Press, 1994.

McNab, W. Henry and Peter E. Avers. *Ecological Subregions of the United States: Section Descriptions.* Washington, D.C.: United States Department of Agriculture, 1994.

McQueen, Jane B., ed. *The Complete Guide to America's National Parks.* 1994-1995 ed. Washington, D.C.: National Park Foundation, 1995.

Perry, John and Jane G. Perry. *The Sierra Club Guide to the Natural Areas of Florida.* San Francisco: Sierra Club Books, 1992.

Ransom, Jay Ellis. *Harper & Row's Complete Field Guide to North American Wildlife.* Western ed. New York: Harper & Row, 1981.

Riley, Laura and William Riley. *Guide to the National Wildlife Refuges.* New York: Collier Books, 1992.

Wernert, Susan J., ed. *Reader's Digest North American Wildlife.* Pleasantville: Reader's Digest Association, 1982.

INDEX

N-O

P-Q

R-S

Waterford Press Series Overview

Waterford Press titles are organized into 14 distinct series based on subject matter, format and price.

Pocket Naturalist® Guides
Flagship line of 400+ species identification guides.

Nature Sets
Packaged sets comprised of three identification guides.

Discovery Series
Series that highlights some of the world's most threatened and critical species.

Adventure Sets
Packaged sets include a wildlife identification guide paired with a National Geographic map.

Our Living Earth Series
Sets of three folding pocket guides to earth and life sciences.

Field Guides
Four field guides that highlight plant and animal species.

Outdoor Essentials Skills Guides
Waterproof folding guides to outdoor recreation topics.

Search & Rescue Guides
Created in collaboration with the National Association for Search and Rescue (NASAR).

The Cornell Lab of Ornithology Waterfowl ID Series
Three guides that address a unique waterfowl ID system.

The Cornell Lab of Ornithology All About Birds Series
How-to essentials and tips for species identification.

Duraguide® Outdoor Recreation Skills
Waterproof guides to outdoor recreation topics.

Pathfinder Outdoor Survival Guides™
Survival guides created with Dave Canterbury.

Nature Activity Books
Activity books with titles for grade levels 2-4 and 3-5.

Disaster Survival Series
Instruction on what to do before, during and after natural disasters.

Over 650 titles with more than 6.5 million sold!

For a catalog, or to order, call 800-434-2555
or visit our website at www.waterfordpress.com